Youth Violence

Other Books in the History of Issues Series:

Youth Violence

Tracey Vasil Biscontini, Book Editor

GREENHAVEN PRESS

An imprint of Thomson Gale, a part of The Thomson Corporation

Detroit • New York • San Francisco • New Haven, Conn. • Waterville, Maine • London

Christine Nasso, *Publisher*
Elizabeth Des Chenes, *Managing Editor*

© 2007 The Gale Group.

For more information, contact:
Greenhaven Press
27500 Drake Rd.
Farmington Hills, MI 48331-3535
Or you can visit our Internet site at http://www.gale.com

LIBRARY OF CONGRESS CATALOGING-IN-PUBLICATION DATA

Youth violence / Tracey Vasil Biscontini, book editor.
    p. cm. -- (History of issues)
    Includes bibliographical references and index.
    ISBN-13: 978-0-7377-2877-4 (hardcover)
    1. Juvenile delinquency--United States. 2. Juvenile delinquency--United States --History. 3. Youth and violence--United States. 4. Youth and violence--United States--History. I. Biscontini, Tracey Vasil.
    HV9104.Y687 2008
    364.360973--dc22

        2007024138

ISBN-10: 0-7377-2877-9 (hardcover)

Contents

Chapter 1: Youth Violence Throughout American History

Chapter 2: Societal Influences on Youth Violence

Chapter 3: Media and Youth Violence

Chapter 4: Responses to Youth Violence

Foreword

In the 1940s, at the height of the Holocaust, Jews struggled to create a nation of their own in Palestine, a region of the Middle East that at the time was controlled by Britain. The British had placed limits on Jewish immigration to Palestine, hampering efforts to provide refuge to Jews fleeing the Holocaust. In response to this and other British policies, an underground Jewish resistance group called Irgun began carrying out terrorist attacks against British targets in Palestine, including immigration, intelligence, and police offices. Most famously, the group bombed the King David Hotel in Jerusalem, the site of a British military headquarters. Although the British were warned well in advance of the attack, they failed to evacuate the building. As a result, ninety-one people were killed (including fifteen Jews) and forty-five were injured.

Early in the twentieth century, Ireland, which had long been under British rule, was split into two countries. The south, populated mostly by Catholics, eventually achieved independence and became the Republic of Ireland. Northern Ireland, mostly Protestant, remained under British control. Catholics in both the north and south opposed British control of the north, and the Irish Republican Army (IRA) sought unification of Ireland as an independent nation. In 1969, the IRA split into two factions. A new radical wing, the Provisional IRA, was created and soon undertook numerous terrorist bombings and killings throughout Northern Ireland, the Republic of Ireland, and even in England. One of its most notorious attacks was the 1974 bombing of a Birmingham, England, bar that killed nineteen people.

In the mid-1990s, an Islamic terrorist group called al Qaeda began carrying out terrorist attacks against American targets overseas. In communications to the media, the organization listed several complaints against the United States. It generally opposed all U.S. involvement and presence in the Middle East. It particularly objected to the presence of U.S. troops in Saudi Arabia, which is the home of several Islamic holy sites. And it strongly condemned the United States for supporting the nation of Israel, which it claimed was an oppressor of Muslims. In 1998 al Qaeda's leaders issued a fatwa (a religious legal statement) calling for Muslims to kill Americans. Al Qaeda acted on this order many times—most memorably on September 11, 2001, when it attacked the World Trade Center and the Pentagon, killing nearly three thousand people.

These three groups—Irgun, the Provisional IRA, and al Qaeda—have achieved varied results. Irgun's terror campaign contributed to Britain's decision to pull out of Palestine and to support the creation of Israel in 1948. The Provisional IRA's tactics kept pressure on the British, but they also alienated many would-be supporters of independence for Northern Ireland. Al Qaeda's attacks provoked a strong U.S. military response but did not lessen America's involvement in the Middle East nor weaken its support of Israel. Despite these different results, the means and goals of these groups were similar. Although they emerged in different parts of the world during different eras and in support of different causes, all three had one thing in common: They all used clandestine violence to undermine a government they deemed oppressive or illegitimate.

The destruction of oppressive governments is not the only goal of terrorism. For example, terror is also used to minimize dissent in totalitarian regimes and to promote extreme ideologies. However, throughout history the motivations of terrorists have been remarkably similar, proving the old adage that "the more things change, the more they remain the same." Arguments for and against terrorism thus boil down to the same set of universal arguments regardless of the age: Some argue that terrorism is justified to change (or, in the case of state terror, to maintain) the prevailing political order; others respond that terrorism is inhumane and unacceptable under any circumstances. These basic views transcend time and place.

Similar fundamental arguments apply to other controversial social issues. For instance, arguments over the death penalty have always featured competing views of justice. Scholars cite biblical texts to claim that a person who takes a life must forfeit his or her life, while others cite religious doctrine to support their view that only God can take a human life. These arguments have remained essentially the same throughout the centuries. Likewise, the debate over euthanasia has persisted throughout the history of Western civilization. Supporters argue that it is compassionate to end the suffering of the dying by hastening their impending death; opponents insist that it is society's duty to make the dying as comfortable as possible as death takes its natural course.

Greenhaven Press's The History of Issues series illustrates this constancy of arguments surrounding major social issues. Each volume in the series focuses on one issue—including terrorism, the death penalty, and euthanasia—and examines how the debates have both evolved and remained essentially the same over the years. Primary documents such as newspaper articles, speeches, and government reports illuminate historical developments and offer perspectives from throughout history. Secondary sources provide overviews and commentaries from a more contemporary perspective. An introduction begins each anthology and supplies essential context and background. An annotated table of contents, chronology, and index allow for easy reference, and a bibliography and list of organizations to contact point to additional sources of information on the book's topic. With these features, The History of Issues series permits readers to glimpse both the historical and contemporary dimensions of humanity's most pressing and controversial social issues.

Introduction

In recent years, youth violence has caused alarm among parents, teachers, and politicians. Though this is not a recent phenomenon, incidents such as the deadly shootings at Columbine High School in 1999 have refueled debate over the causes and prevention of youth violence.

On the morning of April 20, 1999, Eric Harris and Dylan Klebold walked into their Denver-area high school armed with an array of weapons including high-powered guns and homemade bombs. The two, said to have been a favorite target of school bullies, opened fire on their classmates and teachers, killing thirteen and wounding many others before taking their own lives. The case is on record as one of the nation's deadliest school shootings and has become synonymous with youth violence.

In the days, weeks, and years following the Columbine massacre, people searched for the reason behind the senseless act in the hopes of preventing similar tragedies in the future. An investigation into the boys' lives thrust blame at everything from school bullies to violent video games to lax gun-control laws.

Some felt that high-school society played a major role in the boys' attitude toward their classmates. Media reports stated that Harris and Klebold were often harassed and labeled as outcasts by popular students. The pair may also have immersed themselves in Goth culture, a modern movement often associated with rock music and Satanism. Though these associations were incorrect, many viewed the Goth culture as a violent and largely isolating movement. Some also believed that Harris and Klebold were also members of the Trenchcoat Mafia. This group of students, known for their long black trench coats and obsession with guns and the military, publicly distanced itself from the two in the days following the shootings. Group members claimed that the boys were only acquaintances and not a part of the organization. In an interview with the *Denver Rocky Mountain News* only days after the shooting, one member of the Trenchcoat Mafia defended the group's mission, claiming that members were merely "computer geeks" and not at all interested in weapons.

As the search for answers continued, many blamed the media for the Columbine massacre. Some contended that violent music, movies, and video games had desensitized Harris and Klebold and caused them to confuse fantasy with reality. Authorities discovered that Harris had a Web site that he originally used to track his and Klebold's scores for games like *Doom*, in which players use various weapons to kill demons. Later, Harris used the Web site to list the people and things he hated and to threaten Columbine students and teachers. The parents of a student on Harris's Web-site hit list contacted police, but no legal action was taken.

Harris's Web site also posted the violent lyrics to his favorite music, which caused some to blame rock groups for inspiring him to kill. Others felt that movies were to blame. Interviews with Harris and Klebold's friends revealed that the two enjoyed repeatedly watching ultra-violent movies like *Natural Born Killers*. Many still question the role violent entertainment played in the tragedy.

The issue of gun control also came into play during the course of the investigation. Both Harris and Klebold were heavily armed with guns illegally purchased by friends or associates. Klebold's friend Robyn Anderson, who was eighteen at the time, bought two shotguns and a rifle for the teens at a gun show in December of 1998. Mark Manes, a twenty-two-year-old Columbine graduate, sold Harris and Klebold a handgun. After the massacre, Manes went to jail for selling a firearm to a minor, but Anderson was not charged with any crime. According to the law, she purchased the weapons legally, and was therefore free to give the weapons to whomever she chose.

This loophole prompted lawmakers to propose several bills to make it more difficult for minors to obtain guns. It also initiated a storm of criticism against gun shows for selling weapons without first performing background checks.

Five years after the incident, the Federal Bureau of Investigation (FBI) issued its own statement on Harris and Klebold's motivation. After carefully examining the boys' personal journals, videos, and correspondences, the agency argued that Harris was a "psychopath" with a "superiority complex." It classified Klebold as a "depressive" with "suicidal" tendencies who followed Harris's every move. FBI investigators concluded that Klebold might have benefited from medical or psychological intervention, but determined Harris to be "without a conscience" and beyond the influence of rational people.

While many outside influences may have contributed to the massacre, no one cause can be singled out as the root of this tragedy—a conclusion that is also true of the larger issue of youth violence. Though many factors may be to blame, youth violence is a complex issue that is without easy explanations or solutions.

A Violent History

Though many believe that violence among young people is a problem of modern times, society has been dealing with violent juveniles for centuries. In an article for the *Chicago Tribune*, Richard Phillips notes that episodes of youth violence have been prevalent throughout history from the Biblical accounts of Cain and Abel to the frontier tales of Billy the Kid. He argues that, while youth violence is not necessarily more common today than in the past, modern media brings it to the public's attention in ways that were not possible before.

Less publicized incidents of youth violence in the United States occurred during the American Revolution, when young immigrants formed gangs. While the original intent of these gangs was socialization, violence later erupted among the groups. A similar situation occurred during World War II when groups of unsupervised juveniles prowled the streets in order to "defend" their neighborhoods. This spike in the incidence of youth violence captured the attention of those in power.

In the 1920s, FBI director J. Edgar Hoover called on the parents of American children to guide them away from lives filled with violence. Still, many parents contended that poverty was a major factor and that the children of middle- or upper-class families were not victims of such violence. This perception proved to be untrue in 1924 when wealthy Chicago teenagers Nathan Leopold and Richard Loeb murdered fourteen-year-old Bobby Franks. While the motivation for similar crimes was money or power, Leopold and Loeb said they committed the murder for the sheer thrill of it.

Though the case changed some perceptions about youth violence, small-town America still believed its children were safe. The rash of school shootings in the late 1990s shattered this notion. Cases like the deadly school shooting in a rural community outside of Jonesboro, Arkansas, showed the nation that youth violence is a far-reaching issue that is not limited to a certain generation or group. This knowledge has led many to search for factors that influence violent behavior in youth.

Society's Impact

Many blame American society and the environment in which children are raised for youth violence. Some researchers theorize that discrimination may be at the root of violence among young people as it was in Boston and New York during the 1940s when gangs terrorized Jewish adolescents. However, author Williams E. Cross Jr. points out that discrimination brought about by slavery is not the only cause of criminality among young African Americans. Cross argues that the lower standard of education offered to blacks once slavery was abolished significantly contributed to violent behavior among African American youths.

War and political tensions have also caused youth violence. In the late 1960s and early 1970s, frustrations over the Vietnam War divided America. Students at schools across the country protested President Nixon's expansion of the war. While many protested with peaceful displaces, some demonstrations turned violent, the most chilling of which was the shooting of thirteen students by members of the Ohio National Guard, which was sent to keep the peace. The deaths of four of these students led to even more violence on school campuses.

Some argue that the breakdown of the American family and the increase in single-parent households in the 1980s created a generation that is more likely to act out through violence. Researchers have also pointed out that American children's easy access to guns is without a doubt a contributing factor. The 1990 Youth Risk Behavior Survey showed that of the students polled, one in twenty high-school seniors had carried a firearm at some time during the thirty days preceding the survey. Even the economy has been blamed for youth violence.

Author Mike Males feels that youth violence has little to do with a generation of kids out of control and more to do with the fact that many American children grow up in poverty. Males notes that children from poor backgrounds are more likely to become involved in crime, but the elimination of child poverty is largely overlooked by the government as means of reducing incidents of youth violence.

Violence in the Media

While a myriad of factors may actually be responsible for youth violence, people most often blame the entertainment media for inspiring violence. Though some might argue television shows, movies, and video games have only recently become violent, debates about the violent content of such entertainment has taken place for decades. In 1954, people feared that the violence portrayed in comic books was creating a nation of juvenile delinquents. Testimony from experts even led to the regulation of comic-book content, which continued for several decades. Governmental concern continued into the 1970s when a Senate Committee on the Judiciary report cited violence in the media as a major contributing factor to youth violence.

Over the years, different aspects of the media have received more blame for youth violence than others. In the 1980s, attention shifted from comic books and movies to a new genre of music that was quickly growing in popularity. Critics believed that the messages in rap music made violence appear "cool." While author Ivette Yee argues that references to violence in hip-hop music are merely a creative expression of cultural experiences, many still contend that lyrics about violence, sex, and drugs may cause youth violence. In 1985, a group of four mothers formed the Parents Music Resource Center (PMRC). The group's main objective was to establish a ratings system for music and make it more difficult for children to buy music featuring explicit content. A Senate hearing on the issue was even assembled, during which many musicians and experts testified. Before the hearing ended, the Recording Industry Association of America agreed to include a parental advisory label to warn parents of albums with explicit content. The label is still used today, though the rules regarding what is considered "profane" are extremely arbitrary.

Television has also come under fire for increasing the violent content in shows marketed toward children. Though studies conducted in the 1990s suggested that exposure to violence on television was more likely to make children act aggressively, many networks refused to revamp their programming. In his book *Stop Teaching Our Kids to Kill*, Lt. Col. Dave Grossman argues that shielding children from shows featuring violent content is necessary to prevent them from becoming desensitized to violence.

As new technologies emerge and change the way people are entertained, these technology also are scrutinized as causing youth violence. In recent years violent video games in which players rob and kill other characters have been the focus of many critics' attention. There have even been several criminal cases in which the accused was said to have acted out parts from his favorite video games in real life, sometimes with deadly results. While many in the general public believe that these games blur the lines between fantasy and reality, many gamers do not accept this argument. Sixteen-year-old video game player Ron Wilburn feels that most teens understand that video games are a form of fantasy and real-life violence is something having terrible consequences.

Like video games the Internet has also come under fire, but for very different reasons. When schools across the country cracked down on bullying in the classroom, teachers and administrators believed their students were in a safer, less-stressful environment. In many situations, however, the bullying did not stop, but just changed shape. Today, bullies use instant messaging and personal blogs to harass and humiliate their targets. The Internet allows bullies to torment their victims twenty-four hours a day. Recent reports suggest that the problem has gotten so bad in some schools that several teens have tried to commit suicide after enduring almost constant harassment.

Dealing with Violent Youths

The responses to youth violence and the methods used to deal with it have varied greatly over the years. America's first juvenile court was established in Chicago in 1899 to hear cases against children under the age of sixteen. This court, like today's courts, questioned what type of punishment is suitable for our nation's youngest criminals. In 1909, the Juvenile Psychopathic Institute was established to study cases of juvenile delinquency. Researchers at this institute noted that since not all children who commit crimes come from unhealthy environments, some might be suffering from mental disorders requiring medical attention, not punishment.

While the study helped mental health professionals understand the adolescent mind, it did little to influence how adolescents were treated in the juvenile justice system. For many years the courts treated all transgressions by minors, no matter how serious, in similar manners. However, as author Franklin Zimring points out, recently the court has become tougher on youthful offenders by issuing harsher sentences for more serious crimes and allowing more adolescents to be tried as adults. More courts base their rulings on the nature of the crime instead of the age of the offender.

Some communities have addressed the issue of youth violence by going to what critics call "extremes" to prevent violence before it can occur. In the early 1990s, a California town overrun with gang violence sought an injunction making it illegal for gang members to associate with one another in public or wear gang-related paraphernalia. The injunction was passed and the citizens of the community were able to reclaim their neighborhood. Though residents were pleased to see a decrease in violence and crime, many questioned whether such a law infringed on the individuals' Constitutional rights.

The debate over the severity of punishments handed down to youthful offenders has raged on for decades. Some argue that when adolescents commit a serious crime, they give up their right to leniency and should be punished as adults. Others maintain that young people deserve special consideration because of their age. This distinction is critical in cases involving the death penalty, as it was in *Thompson v. Oklahoma*. In 1988, the Supreme Court heard the case of William Thompson, who at the age of fifteen murdered his brother-in-law.

Because of the brutality of the case, the prosecution asked that Thompson be tried as an adult. This request was granted and Thompson was later convicted and sentenced to death. Thompson's lawyers appealed the decision and the case was brought to the U.S. Supreme Court. The court found that capital punishment for a fifteen-year-old to be "cruel and un-usual punishment" that violated Thompson's Eighth Amendment rights.

A similar case was heard in 2005, when lawyers for Christopher Simmons argued for clemency for their own client. In 1993, a then seventeen-year-old Simmons and two other teenagers viciously murdered Shirley Crook and dumped her body off a bridge. Simmons was tried as all adult and sentenced to death before he turned eighteen. Appeals to the state Supreme Court had been rejected until a ruling in the case of *Atkins v. Virginia* stated that it was unconstitutional to execute the mentally ill. Because of this ruling, the supreme court of Missouri decided to hear Simmons' case again and eventually overturned the lower court's ruling, removing the death sentence. The state of Missouri appealed this ruling to the U.S. Supreme Court. In March of 2005, the court ruled that it was unconstitutional to execute anyone under the age of eighteen, thus abolishing the use of capital punishment for juvenile offenders. Greenhaven's *History of Issues: Youth Violence* addresses the complex and often heated debate over what causes youth violence, how it might be prevented, and how society deals with our nation's youngest criminals.

CHAPTER 1

Youth Violence Throughout American History

Chapter Preface

The problem of youth violence is usually viewed as a modern one that is often linked to the dissolution of the American family, the increase in the availability of weapons, and the graphic images children are exposed to in the media. However, youth violence is not simply a contemporary problem that can be blamed on societal influences.

Some researchers argue that examples of violence among young people have existed almost since the beginning of time. Cain was supposedly still a young man when he slew his brother Abel during Biblical times. Adolescent warriors, like Joan of Arc and Alexander the Great, led thousands of troops into battle centuries ago. Jesse Pomeroy became the youngest American to be convicted of murder back in the late nineteenth century, long before violent movies and video games even existed.

Youth gangs have been a cause for concern in America almost since the nation's birth. During the period after the American Revolution and World War II, groups of youth gangs started forming around large cities. Most of the time these groups were ethnic in nature and many of them argued that they were simply trying to protect their neighborhoods.

During the 1920s, two teens from Chicago shocked the nation when they brutally murdered a young boy. Though many young killers had come before them, Nathan Leopold and Richard Loeb's murder of young Bobby Franks brought the problem of youth violence to the public's attention in a way that it never had been before.

The media latched onto the story calling it "The Crime of the Century." Some believe that the ability of twentieth century reporters to bring the news to people quickly is one of the reasons that youth violence seemed to become more prevalent in the last hundred years. In the past, news of these crimes could take weeks or even months to be circulated and even then certain events were surely lost or forgotten.

However, this supposed increase in crime was not lost on many politicians and government officials of the time. The former director of the Federal Bureau of Investigation (FBI), J. Edgar Hoover, called on American parents to help guide their children away from lives of crime and violence. Similar messages were echoed over the next several decades, as the problem of youth violence only seemed to increase towards the end of the 1900s.

Even more attention was given to the problem when a rash of school shootings during the late 1990s sent shockwaves across the nation. At the time, blame for the violence was being placed on everyone and everything, but no root caused could be singled out. These examples help to prove that the problem of youth violence is one that has a much longer history than many realize and is one that has changed over the years.

Youth Violence Occurred in Biblical Times

Richard Phillips

In the 1970s, many people were concerned about the number of criminal cases involving young people. From protests of war that turned deadly to crime for monetary gain, many thought that there was something inherently wrong with modern youths. Others argued that they were no worse than the adolescents of the past. In the following article, Richard Phillips asserts that youth violence is nothing new and has been around since the beginning of modern times. Phillips examines examples of youth violence stretching as far back as Biblical times. The author cites several historical examples of violent youths, including Alexander the Great and Billy the Kid. Phillips questions the assumption that modern youth are really more violent or dangerous than their murderous predecessors. The author also questions several experts about the prevalence of youth violence in modern society. Phillips concludes that young people are no more violent than the children of the past, but that people's perceptions of youthful crimes have simply changed over the years, making them increasingly more sensitive to violence perpetrated by young people. Phillips' work has appeared in the Chicago Tribune.

In the beginning, or almost then, there was Cain and Abel. And there was mayhem.

Cain slew Abel in a fit of sibling jealousy. Ever since, violence has been tolerated as a human condition, even among those of tender age.

History and religion have recorded some of the young notables, passing their deeds along to children of countless generations.

Richard Phillips, "Our Violent Youth: Following in Cain's Steps," *Chicago Tribune*, March 11, 1979, pp. 1, 5. Reproduced by permission of the author.

David, for instance, was little more than a child when he toppled Goliath with a stone.

The Persians were demolished at Chaeronea by Alexander, an 18-year-old Macedonian.

Joan of Arc was 17 when she led French soldiers against the English at Orleans. Bonnie Prince Charlie was 14 when he fought at the siege of Gaeta in 1734.

Then in the New World there was another Bonney, William H.—also known as Billy the Kid. He was 12 when he knifed a man for supposedly insulting his mother—his first victim in a reputed string of 21.

Violence is no less evident today among the young. If anything, it seems more frequent, although certainly less honorable than in other eras, when killing an enemy was proof of manhood.

The young dominate crime reports: Nationally, 73 per cent of those charged with major crimes were under age 25, according to the FBI's annual statistical analysis of bad news [in] October [1978].

Criminologist Franklin E. Zimring, director of the University of Chicago's Center for Studies in Criminal Justice, says:

"However one chooses to measure, crime in the United States is predominantly the province of the young. It is fair to characterize youth violence as a central theme of the politics of crime control. . . ."

Two recent examples: A 16-year-old girl in San Diego says she's bored with Mondays, so she livens it up with sniper fire at a school, killing two and injuring nine. In Cleveland a few days later, a teen-age brother and sister are arrested after hiring an older boy to murder their father.

The news is unremittingly bad, or so it seems. Certainly our middle-class children are more violent.

Are Modern Kids Really Any Worse?

Not according to some eminent psychiatrists and psychologists who specialize in youth, including violent children and adolescents. They say our fears may be getting the better of us, despite the soaring climb in youth violence in recent years.

In fact, there's good news to be inferred from all that bad news, they say. It just requires a historical perspective.

"I would bet there is less (youth) violence today than there was 50 or 100 years ago in this country," contends Dr. William J. Pieper, a psychoanalyst who deals extensively with troubled children and teens.

"The difference today is that we are more sensitive to violence. We are more aware of it."

Pieper, on the faculty of the Chicago Institute for Psychoanalysis, suggests:

"Our day may be the best time in history to be alive. For anyone in the middle class in particular, never has there been such a genuine chance on such a large scale to be so introspective."

Not everyone share Pieper's opinion. But he is not alone.

Several other child and adolescent experts agree in at least one respect: The rate of violence among the volatile young is at least no greater than in past centuries.

It's worrisome, they agree, almost epidemic among young black males living in ghettos. And it is aggravated by the availability of guns and perhaps television stories that shovel cruelty into children's memories. But if we thereby conclude that kids today generally are more prone to violence, we likely are mistaken, they say.

"Kids today may indeed be more self-centered, but I don't believe they are more disposed to killing people than at any other time in our history," says psychiatrist David Zinn, chief of adolescent services at Michael Reese Hospital and a consultant to the Institute of Juvenile Justice.

Much of the explanation lies in population statistics: United States population since the turn-of-the-century has almost tripled, to 218 million.

Crime in absolute figures apparently has grown commensurate with the population. But so has our ability to create an unrealistic appearance of widespread mayhem.

Seventy years ago, for example, the news of an emotionally warped 16-year-old girl terrorizing a California schoolyard probably would not have been heard in Chicago or New York. Today, such a chilling tale not only is published prominently in the newspapers; the bodies and the bloodspots on the sidewalk can be seen in color on network news the same day.

"Our awareness of juvenile violence has intensified, largely because of the impact of mass communication," says Richard C. Marohn, director of adolescent and forensic services at the Illinois State Psychiatric Center.

Still, Marohn is among those who believes that the rate of youth violence is no greater than in "the good old days." It may even be lower now, he speculates.

Says Zinn: "There have been other periods in our history where there has been terrible violence among young people. But no one is around today who remembers them."

Nor were they analyzed by the army of statisticians that now records every piddling arrest and back-alley nosebleed. English-speaking society ceased pubic hangings as an entertainment form almost a century ago. Today we perceive conduct as bad when the first punch is thrown, instead of when a back is turned to a Colt Peacemaker.

Documented Cases of Violence Continue to Climb

Still, the documented trend of soaring youth crime since the 1960s does little to bolster a conclusion that adolescents aren't really any more inclined to violence in late 20th-Century western civilization than in the eras of David or Joan of Arc, when bad news traveled by horseback instead of satellite.

Compared to the late 1940s and '50s, it seems that the United States has been injected with violent youth crimes of almost epidemic proportions. (Homicides have doubled, for example.) Nor has the increase been explained adequately, says Zimring.

Just as unaccountably, though, the rate of violent youth crimes began to level off by 1975.

"In the '70s, we have been holding at a stable but high rate of youth violence," Zimring says.

Whether the rate of violence among youth will continue is moot. Crime tends to ebb and flow, which might explain some of the previous 15-year spurt. Zimring says it already has declined slightly.

In a book about to be published, "The Psychological World of the Juvenile Delinquent," written with Marohn and Eric Ostrof, psychiatrist Daniel Offer traces youth behavior over the last 50 years.

"It does not support the claim that adolescent violence has increased," Offer says, adding that it nevertheless is difficult to convince most laymen: "People get very emotional about it at cocktail parties; they talk about being able to walk in Hyde Park at night."

"And today, there is all this publicity about adolescent violence," Zinn says. "The public is much more aware of it than in past years."

All this awareness is good from one perspective. As Pieper says, it creates an opportunity for introspection about life and how to make it meaningful.

Does an Ever-Changing Society Contribute?

But there is a flip side too. According to David Rothstein, an associate professor of psychiatry at the University of Chicago Medical School, our continued exposure to violence—particularly in movies and television, where the emotional impact is greater than the printed word—may be creating a state of fright among the law abiding.

"It may have a great effect among those who see themselves as potential victims," Rothstein says. "Those who are afraid to ride the elevated, for instance, may get that impression from television and movies."

Not much research has been done on the subject. But such a paranola is logical, if one can infer from the obverse: Studies have shown that portrayals of violence have a known emotional effect on those already disposed toward violence.

"It tends to loosen their controls," says Rothstein, who developed an interest after working with inmates in a federal prison in the early '60s, and served as a consultant for the Warren Commission and later the National Commission on the Causes and Prevention of Violence.

After President Kennedy was assassinated in 1963, prisoner anxieties intensified, Rothstein says. "Several expressed relief that they were in prison, because they were afraid they now would do more violence."

A more recent example occurred in the lobbies of movie theaters showing "The Warriors" in several cities throughout the country. The movie, portraying violence among youth gangs, is making big bucks for the producers. But Paramount Pictures curtailed advertising after three murders by adolescents in three cities occurred immediately after they saw "The Warriors."

The news undoubtedly fanned the fire of TV-movie critics who condemn gratuitous visual violence as a major contributor of adolescent and child aggressions.

Brenda Spencer, for instance, the San Diego teen arrested for firing upon the schoolyard, is reported by friends to have been an avid watcher of the TV police thriller "S.W.A.T.," produced by the American Broadcasting Company.

(Recently, the Parent Teacher Association criticized the television industry for producing offensive and violent programs, many of which are geared to children.)

However, Rothstein and a majority of the child experts interviewed discounted the impact of television violence on emotionally healthy young people.

"Children spontaneously have pretty violent fantasies," Rothstein says. "There probably isn't anything on television that is more violent than what the kids in their fantasies create. I don't think television is turning everyone into a bunch of violent monsters."

One who disagrees is Marvin J. Schwarz, a North suburban psychiatrist, who also believes youth violence is explosively on the increase.

"If what people saw on the television didn't affect their behavior," Schwarz says, "we woudn't have a fortune spent on advertising.

"You can't have it both ways: that advertising influences people and the content doesn't," he adds, accusing TV violence of excessive appeal to the impulsive tendencies of adolescents and children.

Almost everyone interviewed, however, agreed that television violence is inescapably a catalyst for violence among children and adolescents already disposed to be violent.

Says psychologist Robert A. Mark, of Northwestern University's Center for Family Studies:

"Where there is a predisposition to violence (such as an abusive parent) . . . then all indications are that television is a great model for violent behavior."

Mark, however, says that a child growing up in a loving family is unlikely ever to turn to violence.

The expression of affection, such as hugs, the willingness of a parent to set reasonable limits on children, and availability in moments of pain, probably guarantee a nonviolent child and adolescent, Pieper says. He calls such parenting an "empathic availability." It works as well in a single-parent family as in one in which both parents are present, he says.

Such parental expressions of affection as physical touching are vital to children, according to Maria W. Piers, distinguished service professor at the Erickson Institute, the Loyola University affiliate that trains leaders in the early child care field.

Without it, children have less of a chance to grow up emotionally healthy, she says, adding that emotionally healthy children do not usually develop into violent adolescents or adults.

"Parents who injure their children, for example, were in all likelihood neglected or abused children who never quite grew up."

Piers has followed with professional interest news reports of violent children, and she sces something missing.

"The thing that surprises me is that there is seldom any reference to their early childhood," Piers says.

Youth Gangs Began After the American Revolution

Stephen Johnson and David B. Mulhausen

When the term "youth gangs" is mentioned many people think of the tough teens that roam the streets of today's cities, usually armed with guns and often associated with drugs. Though youth gangs are a current problem in the United States, they have existed for many years. Some argue that the origin of gangs in the United States can be traced as far back as the American Revolution. In the following article, authors Stephen Johnson and David B. Mulhausen assert that gangs form as a result of the mass disillusionment caused by immigration, both within America and internationally. Globalization has exacerbated the problem of youth gangs, making it easier for gangs to have active members in several countries. Johnson and Mulhausen believe that only localized prevention of gang behavior will stop the longstanding problem. Johnson is a senior policy analyst at the Katherine and Shelby Cullom Davis Institute for International Studies. Mulhausen is a senior policy analyst for The Heritage Foundation.

America's First Gangs

Youth gangs are nothing new. They appeared in New York City and Philadelphia at the end of the American Revolution. Their numbers and violence correspond to peak levels of immigration and population shifts that occurred in the early 1800s, 1920s, 1960s, and late 1990s. Entrenched in American culture, gangs are romanticized in movies while rap artists copy their dress and jargon. However, because of their growing membership and globalization, gangs have become a public security threat that must be addressed.

Stephen Johnson and David B. Mulhausen, "North American Transnational Youth Gangs: Breaking the Chain of Violence," *Backgrounder*, no. 1834, March 21, 2005, pp. 1–6, 13, 15–16. Copyright © 2005 The Heritage Foundation. Reproduced by permission.

Gangs once provided outlets for marginalized youths to socialize, control territory, and release aggression. More recently, some have evolved into informally affiliated international criminal networks. Two predominantly Hispanic gangs—Calle 18 and Mara Salvatrucha—began to proliferate in Los Angeles during the 1960s and now have fraternal links to some 130,000 to 300,000 members in Mexico and Central America and have expanded across the United States to major cities and rural communities on the Eastern Seaboard.

Gang activities range from defending neighborhood turf to armed robbery, extortion, alien smuggling, and arms and drug trafficking. Gangs provide a handy supply of young collaborators for organized crime. Their transnational nature is facilitated by fluid migration across porous national borders, incarceration with experienced criminals in U.S. prisons, and the weak rule of law in Mexico and Central America. Although no hard evidence links them with terrorist networks, transnational gangs are a potential menace to the stability of North American neighbors of the United States. . . .

Ubiquitous Phenomenon

Street gangs have been around since the dawn of civilization and affect nearly every country except countries with totalitarian regimes, where populations have been immobilized and freedom of assembly is constrained. Gangs were known in 14th century Europe, and Americans have complained about them since the early 18th century. Today, they are a growing phenomenon, particularly in the United States.

The number of cities reporting gang problems went from 270 in 1970 to more than 2,500 in 1998—an increase of more than 800 percent. In 2002, the National Youth Gang Survey estimated that there were 21,500 gangs and 731,500 active gang members in the United States, 85 percent of whom reside in large cities. All law enforcement agencies covering populations of 250,000 or more have gang problems; 87 percent of police departments serving populations of 100,000 to 249,999, and 68 percent of police departments serving populations of 50,000 to 99,999, have reported gang problems; and 27 percent of police departments in municipalities of between 2,500 and 49,999 people have had trouble with gangs.

Although sociologists have yet to agree on a definition, the term "gang" generally describes a group of adolescents or young adults who frequently gather, share an identity, use common symbols, claim control over neighborhood territory, and may sometimes engage in illegal activities. Members may number less than a dozen or in the thousands.

Gangs are less hierarchical than adult criminal groups and not exclusively dedicated to crime. Yet within gangs, delinquency far exceeds that of non-gang youth. A recent comparison between gang members and at-risk youths in Cleveland revealed that:

- 44.7 percent of members versus 4.1 percent of non-members reported committing auto theft;

- 40.4 percent of members said they participated in drive-by shootings compared to 2.0 percent of non-members;

- 34.0 percent of members versus zero percent of non-gang members reported intimidating or assaulting crime victims or witnesses;

- 72.3 percent of gang members versus 16.3 percent of non-members admitted assaulting rivals; and

- 17.0 percent of members versus 2.0 percent of non-members committed robbery.

Finally, gangs are becoming more violent and mobile. Handguns, assault rifles, and grenades have replaced brass knuckles and blackjacks. Cars allow members to commit drive-by shootings and recruit new members in other communities and states. Meanwhile, robbery, assassination for hire, and drug trafficking supply a steady income for more organized groups.

Fertile Soil

Unstable neighborhoods, broken homes, violent role models, and access to drugs feed gang growth. Even the media glamorize and encourage violence. The Seattle Social Development Project tracked a sample of more than 800 juveniles from 1985 to the present, monitoring factors that influenced them to join gangs between the ages of 13 and 18. It measured neighborhood conditions, antisocial circumstances in families and peer groups, school problems, and the early onset of individual problem behaviors.

The Seattle project concluded that, as the number of risk factors increased an adolescent was more likely to join a gang. . . .

The Role of Migration

Surges in gang activity often accompany population shifts, regardless of whether migrants are foreign-born or native. During the 19th century, Irish and Italian street gangs proliferated in East Coast cities as waves of European immigrants entered the United States. African-American gangs prevailed in Los Angeles during the 1960s and 1970s as southern blacks moved west. Migrating to survive, such people have little choice but to settle in disorganized, transient neighborhoods.

Foreigners who are unprepared to compete in their adopted society find survival even more difficult. Gangs offer stability, identity, status, and protection for children who have no parents or must spend most of their time on the streets. Wilmer Salmeron Molina, deported from the United States to El Salvador, told *The Washington Post*:

> My mother used to hit me with a belt buckle and wires, and my father didn't want anything to do with me. . . . [The

gang] gave me money, a place to sleep. Maybe it was the wrong step I took, but I had no options.

Following a migrant influx that began in the 1970s and accelerated in the 1990s, the U.S. Census Bureau believes that between 10 million and 12 million undocumented Hispanic aliens, attracted to seasonal work in agriculture and construction, are now present in the United States. Although the vast majority are hardworking and law-abiding, some of their numbers have fueled Hispanic gang growth. According to the 1999 National Youth Gang Survey, the racial and ethnic composition of U.S. gang members is about 47 percent Hispanic, 31 percent African-American, 13 percent Caucasian, 7 percent Asian, and 3 percent other.

International Links

Although notorious homegrown groups such as the Skinheads, Crips, Bloods, and Latin Kings gained national reach by inspiring imitators or by occasionally recruiting in other cities, two Hispanic groups—Calle 18 and Mara Salvatrucha—have drawn on the ebb and flow of Latin American migrants to become a transnational phenomenon.

The Calle 18 (18th Street) gang coalesced among Mexican migrants in Los Angeles during the 1960s after other Hispanic gangs blocked them from joining. It expanded by accepting Central Americans and natives, as well as members of other nationalities and races. It was the first Hispanic gang known to recruit outside its home city and state, seeking out youth of middle school and elementary school ages to help steal, extort protection money, and sell drugs. Mexican and Colombian traffickers now reportedly use Calle 18 members to distribute drugs in the United States.

The Mara Salvatrucha 13 (MS-13) was formed in the 1980s in the same neighborhood as Calle 18, but among new Salvadoran migrants. At the time, conflict and high unemployment inspired an exodus of Central Americans to other countries.

In the case of El Salvador, a 12-year civil war between communist guerrillas and a fledgling democratic government displaced nearly 1 million people, about half of whom are believed to have entered the United States. Some were former guerrilla recruits from Salvadoran slums who brought with them knowledge of weapons, explosives, and combat tactics. Since its inception in California—and later in Washington, D.C., where another sizable Salvadoran community blossomed—MS-13 has spread to neighboring states, where gangs now prey on and recruit other Latino migrants.

Fueling the Fire

After free elections brought peace to Nicaragua in 1990 and a negotiated settlement ended El Salvador's conflict in 1992, the United States started sending Central American refugees and migrants home. The U.S. Immigration and Naturalization Service deported 4,000 to 5,000 people per year to El Salvador, Guatemala, and Honduras. According to official figures, roughly one-third of these individuals had criminal records and had spent time in American prisons. In 2003, the United States forcibly removed a total of 186,151 persons, including 19,307 who were returned to these three countries; 5,327 had criminal records—three to four times the number deported in the early 1990s. A relatively minor phenomenon in the 1980s, gangs now number between 150,000 to 300,000 members in El Salvador, Guatemala, Honduras, and Nicaragua, although no one knows the exact figure.

At first, the U.S. government sent deportees home without ensuring that there were local programs to receive them. Many knew little Spanish and had no ties to Central America except for having been born there. In El Salvador, jails were already packed with ex-soldiers and demobilized guerrillas who had turned to crime in the absence of employment. As a consequence, many returnees sought out the urban slums and rural war zones that their parents had abandoned in the 1980s.

There, they introduced local toughs and former combatants to the drug-based crime that they had known in the United States. Deportees arriving in Guatemala and Honduras followed similar patterns. . . .

Global Reach

Increasing flows of undocumented migrants across porous borders, deportations, and improved transportation and communication networks have helped the Salvatruchas and Calle 18 to become international. According to Salvadoran police, 90 percent of deported gang members return to the United States as fast as they can. Los Angeles remains their major hub of activity, and Washington, D.C., is the next largest center. In fact, gang members number between 3,000 and 4,000 in Fairfax County, Virginia, alone. Allied groups are present along the Eastern Seaboard from New York to the Carolinas. . . .

Upping the Ante

North America's youth gang phenomenon will never be eliminated or drastically curtailed without harsh limits on civil liberties, larger prisons, or detention programs that rival concentration camps—remedies that are seen as expensive and abhorrent in free societies. *Mano dura* laws that imprison youths for simply wearing tattoos have already been cited as violating civil liberties. Labeling these youths terrorists in the United States may close doors to rehabilitation and give them a political cause, advancing a self-fulfilling prophecy.

On the other hand, piecemeal prevention and suppression merely nibble around the edges of the problem. Program evaluations suggest that no single approach works well by itself or in all communities. Moreover, efforts need to be sustained as long as conditions that lure juveniles into gangs exist. Transnational gangs will continue to flourish as a byproduct of larger social and economic processes such as the growth of transient, unstable neighborhoods and the expanding numbers of undocumented migrants who live on the margins of society. Though unintended, past uncoordinated deportations and subsequent frequent returns to the United States appear to have facilitated the spread of criminal networks. . . .

An Ongoing Problem

Like crime, youth gang activity can be reduced but never eliminated. Because it is neither hierarchically organized nor motivated by politics, it does not currently challenge U.S. national defenses. However, its transnational nature is worrisome, and it is enough of a problem in nearby countries that are still making the transition to democracy that it could destabilize them. Moreover, history shows that disaffected youth were a source of guerrilla recruitment in past conflicts that the United States felt compelled to help quell. The U.S. can reduce this threat now by focusing domestic efforts on the systems and factors that feed it.

Because the phenomenon is transnational, U.S. efforts to curb criminality must have similar reach. In fact, the United States and its North American neighbors should plan for increased trouble. Migrants from South America are beginning to show up in youth gangs, and as political and economic advances stagnate on that continent, the exodus could multiply.

Not long ago, Latin America seemed distant to most U.S. citizens. Now most countries are a plane ride away, roads and power grids crisscross borders, and trade has flourished. As a result of this new proximity, problems that plague more distant hemispheric neighbors will affect U.S. citizens as well. They must not be ignored.

Leopold and Loeb: "Crime of the Century"

Richard Jerome

Richard "Dickie" Loeb, 18, and Nathan Leopold Jr., 19, were wealthy, intelligent college students who seemed to have the best of everything. In 1924, no one would believe that two handsome boys from well-bred families could be capable of committing a violent crime, much less a murder. But the two shocked the nation with their grisly, premeditated murder of an innocent fourteen-year-old boy named Bobby Franks. In the following article, author Richard Jerome explores what came to be known as the "crime of the century" by many historians. The two young killers struck the boy in the head with a chisel, choked him with a cloth, and poured acid on his face to disfigure him. They later dumped his body in a park. Viewing the murder as an intellectual exercise, Loeb and Leopold didn't think they could be caught. They eventually confessed to the murders, however, and were sentenced to life in prison plus ninety-nine years. Loeb was later murdered in prison, but Leopold was paroled in 1958 and went on to live a successful life in Puerto Rico. Jerome argues that though the murder was committed over eighty years ago, the brutality of the crime and the age of the killers still seems to horrify people to this day. Jerome's work has been featured in Time Magazine.

Crime of the Century

To his ghastly misfortune, 14-year-old Bobby Franks umpired a baseball game at Chicago's exclusive Harvard School for Boys on May 21, 1924. Afterward, he was walking home when he accepted a ride from his distant cousin Richard Loeb, 18,

Richard Jerome, "Playing For Keeps: Teenage Child-killers Leopold and Loeb Saw Murder as a Game for Superior Minds," *People Weekly*, vol. 51, no. 22, June 14, 1999, p. 141.

and Nathan Leopold Jr., 19, both University of Chicago post-graduate students who, like Franks, came from wealthy Jewish families on the South Side. What happened next, most historians maintain, was that Loeb struck Bobby four times on the head with a chisel. When the boy "did not succumb as readily as we had believed," Leopold later said, Loeb shoved a cloth into his mouth, suffocating him. After nightfall they took the corpse to a park where Leopold, an avid ornithologist, often went birding. They poured disfiguring acid over the child's face, then forced his body down a drain.

A gruesome landmark in the annals of American crime, the murder became the first of several notorious cases to be designated Crime of the Century. . . . Leopold and Loeb remain symbols of senseless killing. "It captured the nightmare imagination of the country—because it was so cold-blooded, because it was children killing children," says author Geoffrey Cowan, comparing it to the . . . slaughter at Columbine High School. "It seemed so hard to believe."

The case also secured Clarence Darrow's place as one of the most skilled attorneys of his or any other era. After persuading the boys to plead guilty, he focused his efforts on saving them from execution. His impassioned plea brought tears to the eyes of the judge and spurred a national debate on the morality of the death penalty. "You may hang these boys," Darrow told Judge John Caverly. "But in doing it you are making it harder for every other boy who in ignorance and darkness must grope his way through the mazes which only childhood knows." The killers got life plus 99 years.

Why They Did It

Given their economic and intellectual background, Leopold and Loeb seemed unlikely murderers. Leopold had a 200 IQ and spoke five foreign languages. Loeb was reportedly the youngest-ever graduate of the University of Michigan. Evidently, the pair saw the crime as an intellectual exercise, though a misplaced infatuation clearly played a role as well. Scion of a shipping family, "Babe" Leopold was a University of Michigan freshman when he became smitten with roommate "Dickie" Loeb, the brash, handsome son of a Sears, Roebuck vice president. Enamored of Nietzsche's theory that some men are inherently superior, Leopold idolized Loeb ("I felt myself less than the dust beneath his feet," he later said). If not actually gay, Dickie did see an opportunity to form a partnership in a quest that had obsessed him since boyhood: committing the perfect crime. As a court psychiatrist put it, "Leopold acquiesced in Loeb's criminalistic endeavors" and received "biological satisfactions" in return. "I had not then learned to control the fierce emotions of adolescence," Leopold later wrote. "I did what he wanted."

Events Leading to Arrest

In the fall of 1923 the two began plotting. They would kidnap and kill a rich child, then collect a $10,000 ransom. On May 21, 1924, Leopold used a false name to rent a blue Willys-Knight touring car, much like his own red one. Then he and Loeb drove to the Harvard School in search of a boy from their list of potential victims. One of them, Armand Deutsch, then 11, is alive today because he had a dentist appointment that afternoon. "I would have jumped in a car with them in a minute," says Deutsch, 86, a writer. Leopold and Loeb stalked another target but lost track of him. Then Bobby Franks came by.

After the boy was killed, Leopold called Bobby's parents to say their son had been kidnapped, then mailed a ransom note. But when the next day's papers revealed that Bobby's body had been found, he and Loeb abandoned their scheme. Feeling safe, Leopold was stunned on May 29 when he was called in for questioning. At the spot where the body was discovered, a pair of eyeglasses had been found. Only one local firm sold that brand, and just three people had bought it. One was out of the country, and a second still had her pair. The third was Leopold. Babe said the glasses must have fallen from his pocket while he was bird-watching that day. Reciting the alibi he and Loeb had devised, he added that after birding they had picked up two girls and gone cruising in Leopold's red Willys. But evidence mounted against them. A family chauffeur had worked on Leopold's car all day on May 21. Then two reporters compared the type on the ransom note to Leopold's term papers and found that certain letters matched. Loeb confessed, followed by Leopold—though each said the other had swung the chisel.

Life in Prison—and Beyond

In prison at Joliet and later Stateville, Ill., the two remained close and started an education program for inmates. On Jan. 28, 1936, they shared a breakfast of sweet rolls, then corrected papers. But that noon Dickie was killed, slashed more than 50 times in the shower by a razor-wielding inmate who claimed Loeb had made a sexual advance. Leopold was at the prison hospital to say goodbye. "He had been my best pal," he wrote. "In one sense he was also the greatest enemy I have ever had."

In later years, Leopold made a concerted effort to prove he had been rehabilitated. He taught, worked as an X-ray technician and volunteered for a World War II malaria experiment. He also wrote an autobiography, *Life Plus 99 Years*. In time, polls favored Leopold's release, and allies such as poet Carl Sandburg lobbied on his behalf. He was paroled at last in March 1958. Leaving prison with lawyer Elmer Gertz, Babe vomited. "He hadn't been in a car in 34 years," says Gertz, 92. "He got nauseous."

Two days later, Leopold landed in Puerto Rico, where he had been offered work, and a new life, as a lab technician at the Church of the Brethren hospital. "I told him he was two days old when he came to Puerto Rico," says retired Judge Angel Umpierre, 94, then head of the island's parole board. Given an apartment and a $10 monthly stipend (he lived off a modest inheritance), Leopold performed a range of community work. "He was a tremendous individual with the talent of opening people's hearts," says John Forbes, 72, a hospital colleague. "He was good with children," adds Elsa Groff, 75, then head nurse. Indeed, the celebrated child-killer was known as Mr. Lollipop for the treats he gave young patients. Leopold earned a master's in social work at the University of Puerto Rico and also wrote a book on the island's birds. Still, he chafed under parole restriction—he had a curfew and couldn't drink or drive. Says Gertz: "He just hated authority."

In February 1961, at 56, Leopold married Gertrude "Trudi" Feldman Garcia de Quevedo, an American-born widow he had met at a Passover seder. "They were pretty affectionate," says a friend. "But he didn't lose his sexual orientation." Freed from parole in 1963, Leopold traveled the world. On Aug. 30, 1971, wracked by diabetes and heart disease, he died at 66 in a hospital near San Juan. Late in life, Leopold had assiduously avoided discussing his crime. But for many years the photos of two men were displayed in his apartment. One was Clarence Darrow. The other was Richard Loeb.

"Lost" Generations Must Be Saved

J. Edgar Hoover

The Great Depression was a time of uncertainty and despair in the United States. It was also a time that saw an increase in crime, especially among America's youths. As the director of the Federal Bureau of Investigation (FBI), J. Edgar Hoover witnessed some of the greatest crimes of the twentieth century. But one problem in particular plagued him: the number of crimes committed by youthful offenders during that time. Though many argued that criminals could be reformed in the hopes of later reentering society, Hoover felt crime and violence needed to be caught and corrected at an early age. In the following excerpt from a speech before the Chicago Boys' Clubs in November 1939, Hoover stresses the importance of parental involvement and early education against crime. In his impassioned talk Hoover calls for a return to the honesty and morals that he feels were once ingrained in every American. Hoover served as director of the FBI until his death in 1972.

It is with a keen feeling of gratification and of honor and with a far keener sense of responsibility that I address the wide-flung membership of the Boys' Clubs of America. The gratification is founded upon something very close to my heart, the realization that day by day there is a greater awakening to the tremendous necessity of building a bulwark against the ravages of crime during the early ages of its potential victims. Once the tentacles of crime have seized a youth; once its filth has soiled the possibilities of a young man's existence; once the dirt and grime of jails and reformatories, of criminal associations and hideouts, the mental stench of de-

J. Edgar Hoover, "Education Against Crime," speech before the Chicago Boys' Clubs Dinner, Chicago, November 9, 1936.

grading influences and companionships have placed their stamp upon the easily molded mentality of youth, there arises an almost insurmountable task for those who labor toward the building of a better citizenship.

Crime is, to a degree, indelible. It leaves vicious scars both for the perpetrator and for the victim. The progress of youth from his first semi-innocent participation in the minor infractions of a street corner gang through the weary course of police stations, juvenile courts, higher places of justice, reformatories, penitentiaries, and perhaps to the execution chamber is such that it seems to contaminate every one with whom the victim comes in contact—the innocent as well as the guilty. . . .

Crime Prevention Through Education

There is no possibility of wiping out crime by trying to reform criminals. The house has been burned down. The tree has felt the blow of the axe and has fallen in the forest. The house cannot be re-erected nor can the tree again point its leaves to the sky.

The only possible way to strike at crime is to strike at it before it is strengthened through affiliations, through associations, through the cunning of law evasion which comes so quickly through association with the underworld. The time to strike is when the youth is ready to be molded into an adult who shall follow one of two courses—the tangled path of crime or the clean, wholesome one of honesty.

The activities of such organizations as the Boys' Clubs of America are of inestimable value in what I believe to be the most important problem of our lives. It is all very well for us to consider whether there shall be prosperity or whether there shall be depressions. It is all very well to plan for the building of homes, for marriage, for family, for savings, for ambitions. Nevertheless, all of this is worthless if the person who so plans is suddenly thwarted by the effects of a major crime.

Our country depends upon the majesty of our laws. If we have true observance for law, then we have a firm foundation upon which to build for the future. If we have wide-spread, undermining evasion of law, then we have chaos. It is the solemn duty of every respectable citizen to work for the building of better youth, of youth fortified by the proper type of education and of moral guidance against false temptations. It is the duty of ordered society to work toward the elimination of the conditions by which crime is fostered and upon which crime thrives. I speak of ignorance, of disrespect for law, and a slatternly attitude of the adult mentality which refuses to understand and to react to the terrible and wide-spread and ruinous effects of crime. . . .

Any nation which must view tremendous crime tolls, which must watch countless death marches to the execution chamber, which must view crowded exercise yards of reformatories and penitentiaries in which one person out of every five is of less than voting age is a nation which faces danger and disgrace. Persons who are little more than children form one-fifth of our most dangerous heritage. It appears inconceivable; yet it is a stark fact that our misguided boys and girls are thieving, robbing, holding up banks and stores and shooting down employees, proprietors, and the police who attempt to capture them. And after all, in the final analysis, whose fault is it that this has come about? Were these children born with a progenital obsession to steal, plunder, or murder? Does some mysterious and diabolical hand take the child from the cradle and place it upon the uneven road of crime? We know this is not true.

America for a time became so loose-moraled, so thoughtless, so lacking in law-obedience that the youngster came to believe that crime was the smart thing, crime the clever way to make money, crime an easier course than that of honest effort and honest living.

This benighted attitude, however, exists in the minds of too many persons of supposed respectability. Whenever we see or meet a person of lax moral attitude; one who sneers at the laws, who tells you that it is easy to get away with crime, it is our duty to make that person an object of our most intense supervision so that his ideas and attitude may be changed. This is especially true in the field of youth. I cannot understand why Boards of Education in our cities, in our hamlets, in our villages and in our towns should be so lax in their contemplation of the dangers of crime. Why, may I ask you, should we teach the ABC's to our children if one-fifth of them can make use of this knowledge only for the reading of censored material in a cellblock? Why should we teach history to a boy or girl whose only history will be that of a criminal? Why should we teach science and mathematics to those who may use them only for the perpetration of crimes against the commonwealth? It would seem that many of the various agencies upon which we depend for safety and progress are somewhere at fault. I include our system of education.

There is no reason why education against crime should not be a primary factor in our common schools. It should be listed as even more important than reading, writing, or arithmetic. The confidence man, the forger, the check writer, the writer of extortion letters, the kidnaper, who types out his own ransom notes on a typewriter—where did he learn the mechanical manner in which to do these things? They were not born within him; they were taught him at the expense of taxpayers in our schools which failed at the same time to teach inexorably and faithfully a proper observance for law and moral governance. It should be a motto of all such organizations as the Boys' Clubs of America that any school which fails to pound and pound and pound upon the fact that honesty is necessary, that honesty is vital, and that crime is filthy, is failing in its task to properly educate the children with whose future it has been entrusted.

A Return to Honesty

There was a time in those old days at which so many of the parents of the present time are wont to sneer, when a boy or girl sat at his desk after school, writing upon a copybook the old maxim that "Honesty is the best policy." Perhaps it seemed a futile gesture but, as dripping water wears away a stone, so did that old maxim, written and re-written, pound itself into the subconscious brain until a boy or girl said naturally to himself, "Honesty is the best policy." It was his bulwark when some tempter came beside him; it was his assistant; a strong right arm about his shoulders when someone suggested the commission of a theft. Instinctively, that old copybook maxim would arise in time of need. There would be the stirrings of warning from the subconscious—"Don't do this. Don't make an idiot of yourself. Honesty is the best policy."

Crime prevention is as simple at that. It is the teaching of honesty, the teaching of straightforwardness, the selection of youth for guidance during the difficult years of his young life. To achieve these results, we do not need theorists and magicians and persons who can create rabbits out of duck eggs. We need rugged honesty. We need to travel on straight lines. We need to meet on well marked highways instead of continuously losing ourselves in a carnival maze of mirrors. There are too many hoity-toity professors who, wandering in a wilderness of fantastic phraseology, attempt to explain the means of crime eradication in a language which nobody can understand.

There is no magic to the formula of crime prevention. It amounts only to honesty in effort, honesty in office, honesty in law-enforcement, honesty in punishment, and the constant insistence upon honesty everywhere about it. It is because parents, educators, and politicians on school education boards have been misled by solicitors into what might be called the newer fields of education, that the old principles to a degree have been forgotten.

It makes no difference how much so-called education can be piled into a youthful brain if one neglects the means by which this education can be turned to useful account. Therefore, let us work toward a strengthening of old foundations. Let us insist upon principles whereby youth is taught to respect the rights of others, whereby youth is educated to the knowledge that one man's property is not another man's property; that the rewards of service, of effort, and of work are the only true rewards; that in the final analysis no one ever succeeded in getting something for nothing. We have had too much of cynicism; we have had too much of eyebrow lifting; we have had too much of sneering and snarling at the old traditions which have done a very good job of carrying this world through many a trying year, and which again can do an excellent job of rescuing it from the morass into which newfangled Mumbo Jumbo of long-winded names for experiments in education has plunged it. . . .

Protecting the Future

It is shameful that we who comprise society are, in the last analysis, responsible for this condition. We have let greed become paramount. We have let the renegade politician entrench himself in heavy populated areas of poverty and ignorance, there to trade alleged gratuities for votes. We have let power concentrate into hands which do not deserve it. We have let city governments get into the possession of a few men who barter the happiness and the safety of the home to racketeers and captains of crime. Our battle, therefore, is to rescue and bring back into our possession the things which rightfully belong to us. It is not an easy task. It is one for crusaders; one for persons who are willing to give of their every effort and to look upon the battle of crime as a necessary part of their career.

One of the great fields of battle is in the American home. There indeed is a place of endeavor where education against crime should be carried on. It is a terrifying fact that many parents must turn to the mirror to find the true reason why their boy or girl has been engulfed in crime. All too often, in the solitude of sorrow, when the heavy hand of law has descended and a chair is empty at the family table, man and wife, if they be honest, must look to each other and they must say "Where did we fail?" For they have failed! They have failed through a lack of the necessary instillation of the right mode of thinking and the right attitude toward the possessions of others. The father whose child hears him constantly talking of gambling, of seeing notorious crooks and envying them for the money they have made, or reading the newspaper and gloating over the fact that some super-gangster has again been able to evade the efforts of law-enforcement officers, is himself committing a crime in that he is guiding his listening child to take the same path which was followed by this super-gangster. He is wittingly or unwittingly painting a picture of romance. He is placing in that child's brain the thought that he can get away with crime; that it can be made to pay and that it is an easier course than that of honesty.

The fatuous mother who would rather play bridge intemperately than stand guard over the morals or the associates of her daughter has no excuse whatever when that daughter, without guidance, without the protection of parental advice, strays into the cheap dance hall or the roadside tavern, sneaks into the cocktail bar; runs with other girls and men of a low moral character and herself finally takes up an existence as the paramour of a crook. Such parents are, whether wittingly or unwittingly, accomplices of crime. They, through their negligence, have opened the door wide to thoughts of thievery and law evasion. They have made crime something to stir the imagination of youth, something to be emulated and it is their fault when that child becomes a member of a neighborhood gang, when he first robs a store, when he then engages in a holdup and when suddenly the terrible news comes that he was the boy who pulled the trigger when the storekeeper resisted a robbery and he is the boy who stands charged with murder.

They may wonder how it happened; they cannot understand it. But they must be made to understand it. They must be made to realize that a home is, after all, a cradle of endeavor. It can be good endeavor or it can be bad endeavor, as the parents care to make it. And we who can think clearly must view the picture of disaster which faces us and consecrate ourselves to the crusade of education, not only for children but also for parents. We must teach them that the future of America eats at their table and lives in their home and is under their protection. Upon that protection rests our future. May we all endeavor to our utmost that this future be saved for cleanliness, for happiness, and for the re-establishment of the majesty of the law.

World War II Impacts American Youth

Eric C. Schneider

Though gang violence is a notorious symbol of the 1980s and 1990s in urban America, the problem is one that has plagued the nation for a much longer time. Gang violence has ignited numerous times in American history, but one of the greatest surges was seen during one of the country's greatest struggles. In the following article, Eric Schneider explains that gang violence in the 1940s was heavily influenced by the restrictions put on Americans during World War II. Adults across the country were busy with the war. Some parents were overseas fighting, while others volunteered their time to help with the war effort here at home. Because so many mothers and fathers were strapped for time, children were often left to fend for themselves. Schneider asserts that this lack of parental guidance caused many children to make mischief. America's urban landscape was also changing at this time. Cities grew more diverse as people pursued many of the jobs left open by soldiers. Schneider argues that many ethnic youth gangs formed in response. As police forces continued to deny that a real problem existed, these factors combined caused America's young people to become increasingly violent. Schneider is an assistant dean in the College of Arts and Sciences and an adjunct associate professor of history at the University of Pennsylvania.

World War II marked a turning point in the discovery of the youth gang, although this occurred gradually. . . .

Commentators blamed increasing youth problems on "wartime conditions." With family life disrupted as older men joined the military and women moved into the workforce, stories abounded of "latchkey children" left on their own or with adolescents who handled adult responsibilities with varying degrees of effectiveness. Migration separated some families as men searched for defense employment, or it threatened to overwhelm boomtown communities and established neighborhoods as migrant families poured in. Even more problematic than rootless adults were the scores of rootless youths, able to free themselves of institutional and familial restraints. . . .

The Focus Shifts

Concern about adolescent behavior initially focused on girls. In the past, female delinquency had been defined largely in terms of sexual activity, and little had changed by World War II. Newspaper headlines warned of fourteen- or fifteen-year-old "Victory Girls" who exhibited their patriotism by picking up soldiers in dance halls, train stations, or on the streets. Girls, rather than their male partners, were blamed for the rising venereal disease rate, which sapped soldiers' health and delayed their military deployment. Prevention focused on controlling female delinquents, and their delinquency remained an issue of paramount importance throughout the war.

Adolescent males who exercised adult prerogatives and threatened to overturn the hierarchy of age and class were another concern. Working-class males, including Euro-Americans, African Americans, Puerto Ricans, and, in the West, Mexican Americans, had money and entered the public spaces of downtown entertainment districts. These young men enjoyed a peculiar freedom that contrasted strikingly with the constraints placed on a wartime society. They had entered a liminal [threshold] stage, not yet adults but no longer children, newly freed from the tyranny of school but not yet fully incorporated into the discipline of work, awaiting word of draft status, newly affluent with their wartime paychecks, and able to participate in the culture of poolrooms, juke joints, dance halls, and all-night movie houses. . . . The mixture of relative affluence, uncertainty, and independence led to adult anxiety.

The Clothes Make the Man

The zoot suit became the most famous emblem of independent working-class youth. Latino, African-American, and Euro-American males employed the hip jive talk of the jazz world, plunged into the pleasures of the nighttime entertainment districts, jitterbugged, and wore zoot suits—outrageously flamboyant badges of youthful freedom. Zoot suits mocked somber military uniforms with their bright pastel colors and defied warnings of wartime shortages with their long coats, broadly padded shoulders, and voluminous pleats. . . .

Most important, the zoot suit, while remembered as a form of dress favored by African-American and Latino youth, transcended ethnicity. At a time when African-American and Latino migrants poured into still-segregated cities, the zoot suit represented racial transgression for whites. Its wearing did not symbolize tolerance, however, as zoot-suited gangs still organized along ethnic lines. Rather, Euro-American adolescents appropriated African-American and Latino cultural forms—including bebop and the zoot suit—as the most provocative way of expressing both the joy of consumption after the long dry years of the Depression and their rebellion against parents, school, employers, and their impending incorporation into the war effort. Young African Americans employed the zoot suit to celebrate a bebop-based culture, reject the color line, and express opposition to the war. . . . This sort of overt rebelliousness, symbolized in the styles of adolescent dress, aroused a response on the part of authorities and the public at large. . . .

Imitating War

Gangs formed a comparatively minor part of this overall picture. The Office of War Information (OWI) reported that adolescents, envious of the adventures of their older brothers and male relatives, had formed "commando gangs" that imitated military tactics, stole weapons, and initiated raids into enemy territory. The OWI also alleged that gangs were responsible for acts of theft, arson, and vandalism, but, surprisingly its report still did not take gangs very seriously. . .

Interethnic clashes, beginning with the Los Angeles zoot suit riots of June 1943, were the second step in the process of discovering gangs. The zoot suit riots—actually attacks by Euro-Americans on Mexican-American youth—followed several months of tension between white servicemen and Mexican-American "pachucos" [flashily dressed youths]. A number of servicemen had been mugged after leaving bars or while looking for sexual liaisons with Mexican-American women, and in the zoot suit riots they gained revenge. Soldiers, painfully aware of their impending shipment overseas, no doubt resented the freedom enjoyed by their rivals. Aided by civilians, they attacked Mexican-American youths, stripping them of their zoot suits, beating them up, and ritualistically cutting off their ducktails. The turmoil lasted for ten days until the military finally declared downtown Los Angeles off limits to servicemen. . . .

These issues were brought home for New Yorkers later that same summer with the Harlem riot of 1943. The immediate cause of the Harlem riot was the rumored shooting by a white police officer of an African-American serviceman protecting his mother. Although the facts of the case were somewhat different, the rumor seemed credible because of accounts of police brutality and a series of shootings in Harlem, in which plainclothes police officers acted as decoys and then shot their would-be muggers. Harlemites' anger at police abuse, at discrimination, at their higher rents for shoddier apartments, and at the color line in general exploded in attacks on white-owned stores and on police. . . .

What Gangs?

The Brooklyn grand jury complained that Bedford-Stuyvesant's "Little Harlem" existed in a state of lawlessness. They found that "many school children have been beaten, robbed and otherwise mistreated on dozens of occasions." Walking the streets after dark had become perilous, and "many fine churches have closed completely because their parishioners do not dare attend evening services." Citizens traveling on subways and buses had been assaulted, and groups of young boys, armed with knives and other weapons, "roam the streets at will and threaten and assault passersby and commit muggings and holdups with increasing frequency." Youths under twenty-one years of age were responsible for most crimes. "These children form into little groups, run into stores, steal merchandise and run away. They break windows; they snatch pocketbooks; they commit muggings, holdups, and assaults." Law-abiding citizens armed themselves in self-defense, thus reinforcing a cycle of violence. The grand jury blamed young, male, African-American migrants for the upsurge in crime. Moreover, as evidenced by the frequent references to problems with "groups," the Brooklyn grand jury was in the process of discovering gangs. . . .

Brooklyn citizens echoed the grand jury's charges about gangs. Louis Schachter, an attorney, wrote the mayor about gangs whose accomplishments included "beating of women, aged persons and children. Purse snatching and petty theft is a common occurrence. These boys . . . are known as The Saints, Falcons, The Bishops, The Beavers, and The 627 Stompers, among other names. . ."

These were the fears not of rabid racists but of citizens—black and white, young and old—who saw themselves as potential victims of gang violence. [Edwards] Cleaveland [chair of a committee for interracial relations] wrote, "We have known of the existence of these gangs and of the terror which they inspire in young Negro boys who do not belong to them." Their voices were stilled, however, by the clamor over race and crime.

Public officials reacted skeptically to citizens' complaints about gangs. . . . The police commissioner was among those who refused to acknowledge the existence of gangs in Bedford-Stuyvesant. Whatever offenses adolescents committed, they were, he argued, the acts of individuals and not of an "organized juvenile crime syndicate." The commissioner admitted that there were "groups of youths who associate together in this neighborhood, but such association is fundamentally no more expression of evil than the association of the members of a parish ball club. . . ."

Building Borders

In neighborhoods where ethnic succession was occurring, existing Euro-American gangs took on the task of defending turf against the in-migration of Puerto Ricans and African Americans. Bradford Chambers, a journalist trained in sociology, was one of the first commentators to note the proliferation of gangs and the increasingly intense nature of gang conflict as different ethnic communities came into contact. Chambers argued that while gangs had a long history in New York, the inspiration for contemporary gang conflict lay in ethnic and religious hostility. Gangs were to be found in many city neighborhoods, but their activities were most charged in borderline districts, where "fear, suspicion and antagonism" predominated. "The gangs in these communities have primarily one purpose—protective security. . . ."

Chambers investigated an area on the Upper West Side of Manhattan near City College that he called "Mousetown." African Americans and Puerto Ricans had breached the dividing line in west Harlem by crossing Amsterdam Avenue and moving west toward the Hudson, and the area's white youths were resisting. "When the traditional colored districts began to expand . . . the white boys' clubs, led by the Hancocks, the Rainbows, and the Irish Dukes, turned to conflict. In adjacent Harlem, the Negro Sabres, the Socialistics, and the Chancellors joined the battle." The key words here are "turned to conflict," as clubs or street-corner groups chose to become gangs and fight against African-American adolescents. This was a classic "defended neighborhood," in which corner groups patrolled the borders and watched passersby and, when faced with the "invasion" of another group, decided to resist. Some white adults, worried about the changing composition of the area, encouraged gangs to attack African Americans. . . .

Gangs responded enthusiastically to adult support by throwing rocks through the apartment windows where African Americans lived, painting swastikas on the buildings, and hurling trash, debris, and paint-filled bottles into the lobbies of apartment buildings. Needless to say, wandering adolescents, both black and white, were subject to attack by different gangs solely on the basis of skin color. The *New York Times* reported that Frederick Teichmann, Jr., a fifteen-year-old pastor's son, was escorting two girls home from services in the Mousetown area, when he was set upon and stabbed by an African-American gang that mistook him for a gang member. (Following what was reported as the "gang code," no attempt was made to rob Teichmann or to harm his companions.) Under such circumstances, many residents, particularly those with children, saw their only choice as to flee. Boys from families unable or unwilling to leave joined gangs because, according to one boy quoted by Chambers in a 1948 article on gangs, "'it's just smarter for your health to belong, that's all.'"

Skirmishes of the variety found by Chambers were common in neighborhoods undergoing ethnic transition. All over New York, Euro-American adolescents forgot earlier rivalries and organized to defend neighborhood boundaries. For example, in the Tompkins Park neighborhood in Brooklyn, African Americans were moving into an area that had been largely Jewish, Italian, and Irish. White gangs had taken over an abandoned brewery, which was both a clubhouse and a fortress to which they retreated when threatened by others. . . .

Uneasy Alliances

The white gangs included the Brewery Rats, the Pulaski Street boys, the Clover Street boys, and the Red Skin Rhumbas, all of whom were bitter rivals. However, "whiteness" provided a common denominator around which the rivals could rally. When threatened by outsiders, the white gangs formed an uneasy alliance that lasted until the immediate threat disappeared. "During quieter intervals the larger group called together to engage in gang warfare splits up into several smaller groups [that] go by different names than does the whole group." This seemed to be a reflection of their essentially defensive posture. . . .

"Real" gang warfare went beyond rumbles featuring chains, bats, car aerials, and rocks. Morrisania, in the South Bronx, was one of the neighborhoods where clashes were getting out of hand. Like other South Bronx neighborhoods, Morrisania had served as a refuge for Irish, Italian, and Jewish families fleeing the tenements of the Lower East Side or East Harlem. Now they felt under siege as Puerto Rican and African-American families followed in their footsteps. Father Banome, a Catholic priest at Saint Jerome's Church, reported, "'I was just amazed at the struggle between them [Irish and Puerto Ricans], the absolute hatred and disregard. It manifested itself mainly in gang fights.'" One such fight in the spring of 1945 between the Jackson Knights, a white gang, and the Slicksters, an African-American one, resulted in the death of thirteen-year-old Jesse Richardson. Members of the Slicksters had stolen a pair of eyeglasses from a member of the Knights, who plotted revenge. When a group of Slicksters approached the corner candy store that the Knights used as their headquarters, the Knights opened fire on them and killed Richardson. . . .

All over the city, but especially in neighborhoods undergoing ethnic succession, gangs were organizing, street-corner groups were transforming themselves into gangs, and adolescents were arming themselves and engaging in bitter skirmishes. . . . The gangs that public authorities could ignore in 1943 had become a major social problem they had to confront. It was clear by the end of the war that gangs were carving up neighborhoods into spheres of influence as readily as Roosevelt, Churchill, and Stalin had divided the world at Yalta. A war abroad had been replaced by a war at home, and public officials and the press were finally forced to acknowledge it.

A Study of a School Shooting

Cybelle Fox, Katherine S. Newman, and Wendy Roth

In the late 1990s, there seemed to be a "surge" in the number of school shootings across the United States. Though many were ready to place the blame on poor parenting skills, bullying in school, or too much violence in the media, some social scientists had other ideas about what might be causing chaos in the nation's classrooms. In the following article, researchers Cybelle Fox, Katherine S. Newman, and Wendy Roth thoroughly examine a case in the seemingly peaceful area of Jonesboro, Arkansas, to see if they could identify the root of one deadly school shooting. On March 24, 1998 two middle school students opened fire on their fellow classmates and teachers. Four students and one teacher were killed while ten other students were injured. The shooters, Mitchell Johnson and Andrew Golden, were only thirteen and eleven years old when they coldly gunned down their victims. Fox, Newman, and Roth looked into everything from the boys' family backgrounds to how they were treated in school to try to discover some sort of reason for this tragic act of violence. Their research indicates that no single factor lead to this heinous crime, but that a combination of factors contributed to the boys' aggressive and violent tendencies. Fox is a Ph.D. candidate in the Sociology and Social Policy department at Harvard University. Newman is a professor of Sociology and International Affairs at Princeton University. Roth is a Ph.D. candidate in the Sociology and Social Policy department at Harvard University and a Fellow of the Multidisciplinary Program in Inequality and Social Policy.

Cybelle Fox, Katherine S. Newman, and Wendy Roth, "A Deadly Partnership: Lethal Violence in an Arkansas Middle School," in *Deadly Lessons: Understanding Lethal School Violence: Case Studies of School Violence Committee*, Washington, DC: National Academies Press, 2002. Copyright © 2002 by the National Academy of Sciences. All rights reserved. Reprinted with permission from the National Academies Press.

On March 24, 1998, in the third and deadliest in a series of recent school shootings in a Southern community, Mitchell Johnson, 13, and Andrew Golden, 11, both students at Westside Middle School in Northeast Arkansas opened fire on 96 of their classmates and teachers. As a result, four students and a teacher died and 10 others were wounded. . . .

The Shooters

Mitchell Johnson was 13 years old and in the seventh grade at Westside Middle School on the day of the shooting. He had only recently joined the school. Born in Minnesota, he lived for a time in Kentucky before moving to Bono [Arkansas] in 1995. His mother, Gretchen Woodard, married three times. Mitchell's father (and Gretchen Woodard's second husband) Scott Johnson, had an explosive temper. According to media reports, by his own admission Scott Johnson was a screamer. While there is no evidence he was physically abusive toward Mitchell, he punched holes into walls and was verbally abusive, but after his tantrums rarely disciplined Mitchell in a way that would teach him what he had done wrong. Mitchell reacted quite strongly to his father's temper; on several occasions, he was found trembling and physically ill in response, and it could take hours to calm him down. . . .

Mitchell seemed to be doing well at Westside. His teachers described him as a normal kid and a good student, who generally made As and Bs. Many of the adults at the school commented on how polite, respectful and charming he was. Indeed, he received commendations for his good behavior. At ease in talking with adults, Mitchell had a reputation for being a real pleaser. His mother was not very involved at the school but there wasn't that much to be involved in. Gretchen came to Mitchell's parent-teacher conferences faithfully and was supportive of the school in its disciplinary decisions. Mitchell was interested in the Bible and attended Central Baptist Church in Jonesboro. He loved music, performed in the school choir, and even sang at a nursing home on the weekends through his church and youth group. He was active in sports including football, basketball and baseball. He had friends and was especially close to his younger brother whom he always looked out for.

But there seem to have been many different sides to Mitchell Johnson, some of which are hard to reconcile with the "model child" aspects of this description. By some accounts, he had an explosive temper reminiscent of his father. Peers and teachers occasionally landed on the wrong side of Mitchell. He got into serious enough trouble to land himself on in-school suspension at least three times while he was a student at Westside Middle School. The first incident came when he was in sixth grade: he got mad and hit a thermostat in the hallway, breaking its glass case. Shannon Wright, the English teacher whom he would later shoot and kill, placed him on in-school suspension for that incident. The following year, Mitchell was on in-school suspension for cursing at a teacher. . . .

Andrew Golden was 11 years old and in the sixth grade at Westside Middle School at the time of the shooting. He had lived in Bono all of his life, and his father had as well. In fact, many of Andrew's teachers graduated from Westside with Andrew's father, Dennis. Dennis and Andrew's mother, Pat, worked as postmasters in a nearby town and were seen by people in the community as hard working people with good jobs. . . . Andrew was very close to his grandfather, Doug Golden, who was well known in the community since he worked for the Arkansas Game and Fish Commission; it was not uncommon to see the two together around town.

The entire Golden family was known for their avid pursuit of hunting. Andrew was taught to hunt at a very young age; he was given a shotgun for Christmas the year he turned 6. Andrew practiced his shooting at the local range and won awards for his marksmanship. . . .

Andrew was also not considered a disciplinary problem at school. He was never suspended and school officials can only remember one significant incident, in first grade, where he got into some trouble. He had brought a toy gun to school, which was taken away from him by a teacher who told him not to touch it. Andrew got another boy to retrieve the gun for him and then, during recess, filled it with mud or a sand and gravel mixture and fired it at a classmate, hitting her in the eye. . . .

Although they came from very different family backgrounds, Mitchell Johnson and Andrew Golden shared the description of having something of a Jeckyll and Hyde personality. Both could be described as very sweet or polite, particularly by their teachers and in school, but they also had a more hostile side. Those who were privy to the sweet side were stunned by the shooting and found it hard to imagine that Mitchell and Andrew could be involved. . . .

The Shooting

The shootings took place on March 24, 1998, a Tuesday. Students and teachers had recently returned from spring break and were talking about their vacations and getting back into the swing of things when Andrew Golden, clad in camouflage clothing, entered the Middle School at approximately 12:35 pm, just a few minutes after fifth period had started, and pulled the fire alarm. At least two students saw Andrew pull the alarm and leave the building. The students told their teachers what Andrew had done, but everyone filed out of the building through their assigned exit routes, as required. The 87 students and 9 teachers who exited the west entrance were met with a hail of gunfire. . . .

On the morning of the shooting, Mitchell and Andrew were absent from school. Mitchell missed the bus and told his mother that his stepfather, who had actually already left for work, would give him a ride. When Mitchell's mother, who was caring for her 2-year-old daughter and babysitting a neighborhood boy, looked out the window and saw that the van was gone, she assumed that her husband still had it. Instead, Mitchell took the van and drove it to Andrew Golden's home. Andrew's parents, who had left for work, had left Andrew home alone to catch the bus on his own that morning, as they had recently started doing. Instead of taking the bus, Andrew hid in some bushes near his home and waited for Mitchell to pick him up. The boys attempted to get guns from Andrew's house, but the majority of his father's guns had recently been placed in a safe and the boys were unable to gain access to them, even after trying to break the safe open with a blowtorch. They took a .38 caliber derringer, a .38 caliber snub nose and a .357 magnum that were not secured and then drove over to Andrew's grandparents' house. They broke into the house with a crowbar and found an arsenal of weapons—a wall completely lined with rifles—secured only by a cable running across them. From the grandparents' shed, the boys found some cable clippers and used them to break the cable and steal four handguns and three rifles. . . .

Mitchell and Andrew fired less than 30 rounds and struck 15 people. One student, Stephanie Johnson, was pronounced dead on the scene and four others, including a teacher, were pronounced dead at St. Bernard's hospital in nearby Jonesboro. Ten others were treated and eventually released. According to ballistics reports and the police investigation, Mitchell fired five shots from a 30.06 caliber semiautomatic rifle equipped with a scope, killing at least one, but probably two, and wounding at least three. Andrew fired by far the most shots and was responsible for three deaths and wounding at least two others. . .

In the days and weeks after the shooting, the media put forth many theories in search of an explanation. . . .

Mental Illness

The easiest explanation would be to believe that these boys were simply mentally ill, that there was something terribly wrong with them that could explain why they did this. We have no evidence to support such an explanation. Psychological evaluations were performed on both Andrew and Mitchell, but we were not allowed access to them. According to some who have read the evaluations, there was no conclusive evidence of mental illness, though Andrew was generally thought to be the "darker" of the two. During the criminal proceedings that followed the shooting, Andrew's lawyer attempted to argue that Andrew was legally insane and incompetent at the time of the shooting. The courts found that juveniles are not entitled to an insanity defense however, and therefore the full argument was never presented in or evaluated by the court. In addition, there is no evidence that either boy was on any form of medication. . . .

Problems within the family may offer one of the more persuasive interpretations for the causes of the shooting in this case, although here, as elsewhere, the evidence is mixed. Clearly, there were serious problems in Mitchell Johnson's family history. His parents were divorced, he had made frequent moves, and he was a relative newcomer to a community that is still thought of as a place where people spend their whole lives. His troubled relationship with his father was a source of much anxiety for him, and the thought of possibly having to live with his father made him feel hopeless. He had suffered repeated sexual abuse, and while it is not uncommon for children to fear telling anyone about such abuse, Mitchell's fears were aggravated by his worries about his father's temper. . . .

In contrast to Mitchell's more clearly troubled family history, Andrew Golden's family background seemed to be remarkably stable. His family was close and they were well-respected long-time residents of the community. In general, his father and his grandmother were involved in his life at school and wanted him to keep out of trouble; when teachers raised minor issues—like Andrew's making other children feel jealous in kindergarten by selecting who could and could not play with a bag of toy guns he had brought to school—his parents were willing to oblige the teachers and have him keep the toy guns at home. Yet his family was overindulgent and generally gave him his way. . . .

Bullying

According to a number of people close to the boys—including classmates, teachers and law enforcement officials—bullying, or at the very least teasing, may have been a factor in the shootings. One of Mitchell's teachers knew before the shooting that Mitchell was being picked on but felt that he was overreacting to his classmates' teasing—that he was being too sensitive. Mitchell liked to brag and when classmates tried to cut him down to size, he would become angry. . . .

Andrew was a slight boy, leading some people to think it is possible that he was bullied. Students said that Andrew had friends, and while he wasn't in any clique, he was not considered a loner. While several students did not have the perception that Andrew or Mitchell were picked on a lot, some classmates did tell adults in the community that they were bullied or teased. However, it does not appear that they were singled out for excessive abuse. . . .

Gun Culture/Culture of Violence

Most of the people in the community understandably resent any representation of Southerners as gun-toting, violent people. Most boys learn to hunt, they admit, but people are generally responsible and furthermore "it is not guns, but people, that kill." Some also argue that guns are prevalent in all rural communities, North and South. The distinction therefore should be made between rural and urban, not between the North and the South.

We found no conclusive evidence to support or discount either claim but it is clear that Mitchell and Andrew were able to access an arsenal of weapons for this crime. While most of the Goldens' weapons were secured—either in a safe or by a cable—Mitchell and Andrew were able to access more than enough firepower for the shooting. While it is impossible to know the impact trigger locks might have had, none of the weapons was equipped with them. After this tragedy, civil suits were mounted by the victims' families against the gun manufacturers and some of them lobbied for trigger locks. Most of the youth we spoke with thought it would be pretty easy to get a gun if they wanted one. . . .

Conclusion

No single cause accounts for the behavior of Mitchell Johnson and Andrew Golden. The cumulative impact of the forces that span the individual, the family, the school and society are all involved. Both boys were troubled. Mitchell had a very difficult and stormy relationship with his father and had a history of sexual abuse, both as a victim and in turn as an abuser. He had trouble controlling his temper and flew off the handle over slights—being teased by peers or being dumped by a girlfriend. These incidents became a channel for a deeper anger. Indeed it is possible that the abuse Mitchell suffered as a child intensified normal adolescent male concern over masculinity that was subsequently reinforced by a real failure with a girl. As we have not seen the psychiatric reports, we do not know whether this possibility has been examined in any therapeutic setting.

Andrew had a reputation in his neighborhood as a menace and was reported to have been cruel to animals; he appeared to many in the community to be spoiled by his family, and some speculated that a lack of discipline at home may have led him to think he could get away with anything. Andrew may also have been teased at school. However, nothing in the disciplinary histories of either child suggested to school officials that these boys were particularly troubled. . . .

While residents in the Westside and Jonesboro communities are still unable to explain why this tragedy happened, they are generally quick to tell us, "If it could happen at Westside, it could happen anywhere." Many urged that school districts, communities, and indeed our nation simultaneously work to prevent and prepare for school shootings. . . .

CHAPTER 2

Societal Influences
on Youth Violence

Chapter Preface

Over the years, many people have searched for some sort explanation for violence among young people. Societal forces, such as poverty and racial discrimination, are often blamed for youth violence.

Some researchers point out that American slavery and the racism that followed have created a society that marginalized many African Americans and led some to lash out violently. However, others argue that it is the substandard level of education and the lack of opportunities afforded to former slaves that has had an impact on generations of young African Americans.

Another factor that supposedly contributes to youth violence is religious intolerance. In the 1940s, gangs of anti-Semitic youths harassed Jewish teenagers in major cities across the United States. Synagogues also became the target of the teens' rage. As messages of hate spread across cities by coalitions of anti-Semitic Christian groups, the police largely ignored the violence against the Jewish community.

Even politics has played a role in the problem. During the late 1960s and early 1970s, many young people were frustrated over the United States' involvement in the Vietnam War. Many called for a withdrawal of all U.S. forces in the region through anti-war protests held across the country. Though many of these protests ended peacefully, others turned violent. The most famous of these incidents was the shooting of several college students during a protest at Kent State University in Ohio.

During the 1980s, an increase in single-parent households led many researchers to believe that there was a link between this phenomenon and youth violence. Supporters of this idea believe that children who grow up without one of their parental figures are more susceptible to become involved in violent acts as adults because they lacked proper role models as children.

As violence, especially handgun violence, began to increase in schools across the country, many saw the availability of guns as a contributing factor in youth violence. Several surveys showed that more students in the early 1990s were bringing weapons to school. Many believed that the only way to prevent future violence was to enforce stricter gun control laws.

In the late 1990s, violence among young people seemed to be out of control. Incidents of school shootings and violence were on the rise and a mystified nation desperately searched for a solution. While violence in the media and absentee parents were often targets for blame, many believed that these kids were simply "bad" and beyond any sort of help that they might be given. However, others felt that the fact that more American teens and children were living at or below the poverty level than ever before had a significant impact on their involvement in crime.

Though many believe that some of these factors do contribute to youth violence, it is probably a combination of many different factors, including societal ones, that contribute to youth violence.

Racial Discrimination Is Not the Only Root of Violence

William E. Cross Jr.

Sociologists have investigated the link between violence among youth and race relations in the United States for many years. Some argue that past injustices against specific groups has led later generations to act out against a society that mistreated their ancestors. In the following article, scholar William E. Cross Jr. explores how slavery and the racial prejudice against African Americans has affected current generations. When slaves were freed after the Civil War, they showed surprising ambition toward educating themselves. This excitement for education was met with racial prejudice; society did not properly fund the education of African American students. This treatment lasted into the mid-twentieth century when the poorest and most overcrowded schools employed "double-shifting," a practice that had teachers teaching two different classes of children per day, a morning class and an evening class. Double-shifting meant African American students spent less time in the classroom than children of other races. Without education to occupy their time, these children turned to mischief. Cross argues that the double-shifting that occurred from 1930 to 1940 helped contribute to the violence among African American youths today. Cross is a professor of social-personality psychology at City University of New York.

The current tendency to see Black juvenile delinquency as having a "life of its own" can be traced back to [E.F.] Frazier's (1939) text on the Black family (Frazier, 1948). In chapter seventeen, titled "Rebellious Youth," Frazier argues

William E. Cross Jr., "Tracing the Historical Origins of Youth Delinquency & Violence: Myths & Realities About Black Culture," *Journal of Social Issues*, vol. 59, no. 1, 2003, pp. 67–82. Copyright © 2003 The Society for the Psychological Study of Social Issues. Reproduced by permission of Blackwell Publishers.

that the Black delinquency rate steadily increased between 1930 and 1940, with greater crime involvement in the more run-down sections of the Black community, where broken Black families resided. He thought this trend became attenuated, as one moved outward to those sectors of the ghetto where more accomplished, intact Black families lived. According to Frazier:

> [A] decline in delinquency coincided with the decline in dependency, family desertion, and illegitimacy in the . . . zones indicating the expansion of the Negro population. The rates were high in those areas characterized by physical decay and the lack of organized community life. In these areas the customary forms of social control, as represented by the family and simple folk culture of the migrants from southern communities, tended to break down or disappear altogether. (Frazier, 1948, p. 279)

Frazier presented cases that underscored the failure of broken or dysfunctional Black families to monitor their children, flooding the streets with a steady stream of Black youth. He weaves issues of poverty and oppression into the discussion, but the emphasis is clearly on problems internal to the Black family and the Black community. More recently, [J.U.] Ogbu (1978, 1991) emphasized the same kind of thinking as did Frazier in viewing high rates of Black crime as emanating from within Black culture. However, new research suggests that the crime rise Frazier observed and to which Ogbu makes reference may have been the result of key structural and institutional problems over which Blacks had little control.

Over Capacity and Under Funded

In 1984, [M.W.] Homel published an important book on the education of Blacks in the public schools of Chicago for the period covering 1920 to 1941 (Homel, 1984). Like Frazier, Homel, in a section dealing with family life, community, and the schools, makes note of the high delinquency rate which often characterized portions of the Black community. However, unlike Frazier, who emphasized the role of community and family dynamics, Homel discovered a more systemic and oppressive origin to Black delinquency: *the schools*. For the same time period stressed by Frazier (1930 to 1940), Homel found that the White ethnic population stabilized and began to decline in terms of percentage of ethnic White children attending public schools. Consequently, by 1940, overcrowding was not much of a factor in the administration of schools attended by the children of White, ethnic parents. The reverse was true for Blacks, as their numbers and the percentage of children in Chicago schools increased rather steadily between 1930 and 1940. In a report dated 1941, which recorded the enrollment capacity of a large number of Black elementary as well as Black high schools, the schools were said to have an official capacity of 18,800 students but the actual enrollment for all the schools was 28,673 or 35% more students than the actual legal capacity. A few of the elementary schools were running 30-40% over capacity, but most alarming was the overcrowding at Black high schools. Du Sable High had an official capacity of 2,400 students but was serving as many as 4,000 students. Phillips High, with a capacity of only 1,500 students, was being asked to accommodate the incredible figure of 3,600 students or an overcapacity of nearly 240%! These figures reflect also the density of racial segregation in Chicago; for the time period in question, Black areas of the South Side of Chicago had 90,000 people per square mile, while for nearby White neighborhoods the density was 20,000 residents per square mile. As Homel underscores, the impact of residential overcrowding was evident in ghetto classrooms.

The Double-Shift Fallacy

Part of the problem was that officials were hesitant to invest in new schools for Blacks, and even with the White school population on the decline, new facilities were more likely to

be built in White than Black districts. With limited invest-
ments in Black school construction, the school board resorted
to other remedies to relieve overcrowding at Black schools,
namely, the use of temporary structures and something called
double shifts (Homel, 1984, pp. 79–80). To maintain school
segregation, officials provided dismal, damp, and unhealthy
temporary structures called portables, *but more important to
our discussion of Black juvenile delinquency rates was the double
shift remedy.* School schedules were altered and one school
might serve two or *more* shifts of students every school day!
Although rare in White neighborhoods, the number of
multiple-shift schools in the ghetto climbed from four in
1931, to seven in 1936, and to thirteen in 1940. Compared to
White students, Black students were spending 20% to 40%
fewer hours in school. At Black high schools where overcrowding was most acute, the situation was nearly impossible.
*For the age cohort most vulnerable to delinquency trends, Black
adolescents were literally being turned out into the streets by the
very institution designed, in part, to prevent delinquency through
educational engagement.* The consequences of this predicament
were predictable:

> School overcrowding . . . hurt both youth and the commu-
> nity as a whole by offering double-shift students too many
> chances to get into trouble. Observers pointed out that the
> shift system made it easy for pupils to become truants. A
> white women's club officer testified, "Any child on the street
> at any hour can explain his presence by saying, 'I went to
> school this morning,' . . . or 'I go to school in the afternoon.'"
> Even youngsters who were dutiful about attending classes
> had, in the words of the civic leader Irene McCoy Gaines, "a
> half day in school and a half day on the street." Children
> from households that had no adult home during the day
> spent their afternoon or morning without supervision. Half-
> day sessions, grumbled one South Sider, allowed boys and
> girls "time to learn all kinds of devilment." Children barred
> from school by seat shortages passed their time on the street

corners, in adult entertainment establishments, and in un-chaperoned apartments. "We have seen dozens of boys travel-ing in gangs for want of anything to do," a black newspa-per columnist reported . . . Journalists, Urban League personnel, and PTA leaders blamed shortened school hours for the ghetto's high incidence of youth crime. As Alterman Earl B. Dickerson asked rhetorically in 1941, "Is it any won-der that our juvenile delinquency rate is one of the highest in the country?" (Homel, 1984, pp. 82–83)

In effect, Frazier's assertion that crime and juvenile delin-quency go hand and hand with a pathogenic Black culture was more about myth making than fact. Frazier earned his doctorate from the University of Chicago and his work on the Black family and Black adolescence was published by the Uni-versity of Chicago in 1939. A great deal of the information that went into the making of his text on the Black family re-flected the observations he made of Black families living in Chicago. How he came to miss the role of school overcrowd-ing and double-shift schools is not clear. It is interesting to note that his chapter on rebellious youth, which was described a few paragraphs back, contains not a single reference or com-mentary about schools or the school system.

Don't Blame Genetics

Today, in a similar fashion, we do violence to Black people in general, and Black males in particular, by accepting as fact that Blacks are genetically predisposed (Duster, 1992) or "cul-turally" primed (Payne, 2001) for involvement in crime, drug usage, and drug trafficking (Lusane & Desmond, 1991). We are so accepting of the Black-crime/Black-culture connection that there is little outrage about the disproportionate number of Black men who have some connection to the prison or pa-role systems (Miller, 1996). Just as Chicagoans in the 1930s and 1940s failed to perceive double-shift schools as a form of racialized-education, so today many people do not view our current penal code as having racialized drug usage (Duster,

1997). National surveys have established that Blacks are no more likely to use illicit drugs than are Whites (SAMHSA, 1997), although crack cocaine is readily found in Black communities while powdered cocaine is found in White suburbs (Duster, 1997). The so-called war on drugs turns on the crack versus powdered cocaine distinction, in that punishment is stronger for crack cocaine arrests than for powdered cocaine arrests, and therefore Blacks are arrested more, because crack is more readily available in Black communities. With the passage of drug laws in the 1980s, upwards of 90% of juvenile drug arrests have involved Blacks (Duster, 1997; Miller, 1996; Mauer, 1999; Tonry, 1996). Not only did the laws create an incredibly differential arrest ratio based on race, but also mandatory sentencing guidelines meant more Blacks would spend longer periods of time in prison. Before 1986, the average drug sentence for Blacks was 6% longer than for Whites, but four years later as the mandatory sentencing locked into application, the average sentence became 93% higher for Blacks (Tonry, 1996). In a few short years, the racialization of drug use and imprisonment became the norm. Duster (1992) points out that in 1983, 63% of the prison commitments for the state of Virginia involved Whites and only 37% involved minorities. By 1989, the pattern was reversed, with new commitments showing 34% Whites and 65% minorities, even though, as we need to keep in mind and as was pointed out earlier, drug usage by Whites and Blacks could not be differentiated, and in some instances it was actually higher for Whites. The pattern found in Virginia has been documented to be true for other states across the nation (Lusane & Desmond, 1991). Even after experts have explained to the general public that the drug laws are racially and socio-economically slanted, there has been little support for changing the laws at either the state or federal levels (Rep. Rangel [D-NY] introduced H.R. 2031, Crack-Cocaine Equitable Sentencing Act of 1997, but it failed to pass). It is as though people are saying that yes, maybe the laws don't help, but the real reason for all those folks in prison cannot possibly be the law itself. This likely echoes what was said back in the 1940s that yes, now that you point it out to me, double-shifting probably does not help matters, but there must be some cultural or genetic reasons why so many Black teens keep getting into trouble. . . .

Unsettled History

If there is a message from this analysis it is that observers who are deeply immersed in the present and who sincerely want to find a way to both explain and solve certain Black problems should not assume that the legacy of slavery thesis is, to borrow a phrase from the study of law, "settled" history. Ogbu's attempt in 1991 to link contemporary Black achievement problems with slavery should never have seen the light of day because, by 1991, evidence to the contrary was abundant. The historical record is there but if it is not studied first hand, one begins the search for solutions to Black problems by committing violence against the history of the very people one professes to want to help. Finally, this analysis suggests that a group's disproportionate involvement in crime does not automatically bring into question the integrity of that group's culture. For example, our analysis confirmed the high rate of Black juvenile delinquency for Blacks living in Chicago, circa 1930 to 1940. However, as soon as it was revealed that for the time period in question, Black adolescents were spending upward to 40% less time in school because of a double-shift policy, then it became easy to comprehend that such a policy was essentially pushing Black youth toward mischief making and the streets, and no amount of Black cultural integrity could have prevented the trend. Consequently, the co-existence of Black crime rates and Black cultural integrity is not a contradiction, when systemic forces neutralize or undermine the *ameliorative potential* of Black culture (Mullings and Wali, 2001).

Anti-Semitic Youth Gangs Were Encouraged in 1940s America

Stephen H. Norwood

In New York and Boston during World War II, Irish Catholic youths began propagating violent anti-Semitic crimes against Jewish youths. In the early 1940s, beatings of Jewish children and vandalism of synagogues began increasing, but the press failed to report most of these incidents. As the brutality of the attacks intensified, with some children being stabbed and having their clothes torn off, newspapers began to report the violence. In the following article, Stephen H. Norwood shows that the violence was perpetuated by a lack of police action and an unwillingness to punish the perpetrators. Norwood points out that since most of the cities' police officers were Irish Catholic men, they were reluctant to punish the youths and labeled the crimes normal juvenile delinquency. The youths later explained that religious coalitions such as the Coughlinite Christian Front had distributed propaganda. Norwood shows that the group spread a message of hate throughout the cities, inspiring young people to commit terrible crimes against their Jewish peers. Norwood is a professor of history at the University of Okalahoma.

In October 1943, the New York newspaper *PM* declared that bands of Irish Catholic youths, inspired by the Coughlinite Christian Front, had for over a year waged an "organized campaign of terrorism" against Jews in Boston's Dorchester district and in neighboring Roxbury and Mattapan. They had violently assaulted Jews in the streets and parks, often inflicting serious injuries with blackjacks and brass knuckles, and had desecrated synagogues and vandalized Jewish stores and homes. *The New York Post* stated that the "beatings of Jews" in Boston were "an almost daily occurrence." State Senator Maurice Goldman, representing 100,000 Jews, residing mostly in Dorchester, Roxbury, and Mattapan, joined by four state representatives from those areas, declared to Governor Leverett Saltonstall that their constituents were living "in mortal fear." Many Jews could not leave their homes, even in daylight, frightened of being beaten by youths from adjacent Irish Catholic neighborhoods like South Boston, Fields Corner, and the Codman Square area, who deliberately entered Dorchester, Roxbury, and Mattapan to go "Jew hunting." The New York Yiddish daily *The Day* called the antisemitic violence that had occurred in Dorchester during the previous year "a series of small pogroms." [Pogrom: an organized massacre of helpless people, specifically Jews]. . . .

In late 1943, New York newspapers reported that vandals had desecrated Jewish cemeteries throughout Brooklyn, Queens, and other areas of Long Island, overturning gravestones and painting swastikas on them. U.S. Attorney-General Francis Biddle compared the damage to New York's Jewish cemeteries to that in Nazi-occupied countries in Europe, an "outbreak of [an] Axis pattern in our own country." New York Congressman Samuel Dickstein charged that the Christian Front was responsible for the cemetery desecrations, and declared that "Not even the dead seem to be secure from organized terrorism."

[In New York] as in Boston, bands of Irish Catholic youths confronted people on the streets, demanded to know if they were Jewish, and beat them mercilessly if they said they were, sometimes disfiguring them. For example, three teenagers in the Bronx surrounded a fourteen-year-old Jewish boy, and when he answered their question in the affirmative, they shouted, "He's a Jew, let him have it!" They proceeded to slash him across the face with a knife, inflicting a deep wound that left a long scar from his ear to his lip. *The New York Post* reported that the assault was only one of many recorded in the previous weeks in the Bronx's Tremont section and in Washington Heights. It noted that Jewish mothers in Washington Heights knew that, every time their children left home, "they [were] walking into potential danger. . . ."

The Christian Front espoused an isolationism that was explicitly antisemitic. Francis Moran often aroused his audiences at Boston Christian Front meetings by asking, "Who are the blood suckers plotting to send our boys to die in England?" His listeners would scream, "The Jews!" In June 1941, Moran denounced the war as "just a racket for the Roosevelt-Rothschild-Lehman families"—that is, Jewish bankers who were allegedly conspiring with the president to force America to intervene unnecessarily in a European conflict for their own financial gain. In June 1941 and again in August, Moran arranged the Boston screening of Seig im Westen (Victory in the West), celebrating the German conquest of France and the Benelux countries. The Boston Christian Front also distributed books and pamphlets for Flanders Hall, the Nazi government's publishing outlet in the United States. . . .

New York City's Commissioner of Investigation, William Herlands, reported that in 1939 the Christian Front had held eighty-six outdoor and seven indoor meetings in a single Bronx police precinct, the 40th, and that the Christian Mobilizers had held forty-two outdoor and twenty-three indoor meetings there. He noted that "rarely did a night pass that the popular corners . . . were not all simultaneously being used as a forum" for the Christian Front and the Christian Mobilizers. In 1944, the *New York Post* described this precinct as "a community torn by hatred . . . intense anti-Semitic violence, vandalism, and subversive activity. . . ."

As in Boston, a significant number of New York policemen were Christian Front members or sympathizers, uninterested in protecting the rights and safety of Jews. *New York Post* columnist Victor Riesel noted in 1944 that Federal Bureau of Investigation director J. Edgar Hoover had several years before supplied New York's Mayor La Guardia with a list of 1,500 policemen who had applied for membership in the Christian Front. The city government never took disciplinary action against any of them. Riesel commented that hundreds of New York policemen had openly fraternized with the Christian Fronters who, before Pearl Harbor, had picketed Jewish stores, businesses, and homes. In 1941, some of the picketed merchants had asked New York Police Commissioner Lewis Valentine to order patrolmen to take action against this antisemitic harassment, but were told that he could not prevent "peaceful picketing." Nearly two-thirds of New York's policemen were Irish American. . . .

Jews, whom many Christians had for centuries scorned for religious reasons, provided a scapegoat for many Americans frustrated by economic setbacks during the Depression, and domestic fascist groups proliferated, with over one-hundred new antisemitic organizations formed between 1933 and U.S. entry into World War II in 1941. The rapid, seemingly irresistible expansion of Nazi power in Europe during the 1930s greatly encouraged these domestic fascists, who like their German counterparts, blamed Jews for all their country's misfortunes. . . .

At the grass roots level, Jews in Dorchester, Roxbury, and Mattapan now organized vigorous self-defense units to protect residents and their property against further assaults. Rabbi Korff announced that public officials' indifference to Jewish safety would cause Jews "to organize their own protective association." Neighborhood air raid wardens and auxiliary police began patrolling the streets to guard against the Irish American intruders, who, as *PM* observed, "rove the area . . . unmolested by police." A group of Jewish butcher boys banded together to protect Jews returning home from Friday night synagogue services. *The Day* noted that many Jewish youths

and army draftees, "spurning the advice to hush-hush . . . answer[ed] blow with blow." It compared Dorchester's Jewish
self-defense groups to those that Jews had organized in czarist
Russia to combat pogromists.

New York Jews similarly prepared to defend themselves.
Jewish parents in the Bronx who attended a police-sponsored
meeting on "juvenile delinquency," the term police used to de-
scribe the antisemitic attacks, rejected the proposal to establish more youth recreation centers put forward by city social
workers. A Jewish mother declared at the meeting, "We'll patrol ourselves. . . . If the police won't protect [our children] we
will." *PM* reported that two-hundred Jewish parents were setting up a vigilante patrol.

As in Boston, Jewish air raid wardens attempted to provide protection for Jewish residents, but, outnumbered, they
were frequently assaulted by bands of antisemitic youths, who
challenged them with the question, "Are you a Christian or a
warden?" Spectators shouting "Kill those Jews" offered them
encouragement. . . .

Government and police officials in both Boston and New
York initially asserted that the violence about which the Jews
complained amounted to little more than ordinary juvenile
delinquency, and claimed it consisted of isolated acts, and did
not form a general pattern. Governor Saltonstall insisted that
the Dorchester situation had never been brought to his attention prior to the week before [Arnold] Beichman's article [en-
titled "Christian Front Hoodlums Terrorize Boston Jews," published in *PM* in October 1943.] Immediately upon reading the
article, Saltonstall wrote to Boston Police Commissioner Joseph F. Timilty that its "conclusions and insinuations against
the people of Boston, its mayor, and the governor of the state
are utterly unfair and without foundation." He asked Timilty
to investigate at once. The police commissioner responded,
"There is no organized activity by the Christian Front or any
group relative to anti-Semitic activities." Timilty disputed

PM's charge that the police were not protecting Jewish residents of Dorchester and Roxbury against "unwarranted attacks." Boston's Mayor Tobin, speaking about the Dorchester outbreaks for the first time a few days after the *PM* disclosures, announced that "it appears to be strictly a juvenile problem. . . ." However, Ruth O'Keefe, a member of the Massachusetts Parole Board and an authority on juvenile crime, declared that gang violence in Boston, which she maintained specifically targeted Jews, was directly inspired by Coughlin. . . .

In New York, Mayor La Guardia viewed the antisemitic "incidents" as "sporadic and unorganized," and the police remained unsympathetic to calls that they take action to stop the violence. In December 1943, New York's Commissioner of Investigation, William Herlands, denied any connection between the "teenage marauders" and Coughlinite organizations. *The New York Post* in late December 1943 noted that, despite scores of Jewish complaints about physical attacks and synagogue invasions in Washington Heights, Magistrates Court had tried no cases related to such offenses during the previous three months. The police inspector in charge of the four-and-a-half-square-mile district, in which 365,000 people resided, claimed there had been only "a few isolated" cases of vandalism involving pre-teenage boys, and that no synagogues had been defiled. The New York police often described acts of antisemitic vandalism as "boyish pranks. . . ."

Attorney-General Bushnell cited, as an example of the "disgraceful breakdown of law" in Boston under Timilty, the arrest and beating by the police of four Dorchester Jewish boys who had been assaulted by a large Irish American crowd. Jacob Hodas, age seventeen, one of the Jewish boys whom police charged with "participating in an affray," testified that several officers, including Sergeant Bernard Fay, had subjected him to a "terrific beating" at the station house, repeatedly striking him with a blackjack until he toppled to the floor, nearly unconscious. He stated that the police had also manhandled at least two of the other Jewish boys. Two Jewish adults testified that they had seen Sergeant Fay push his pistol into Hodas's stomach and threaten to shoot him. Robert Ruttenberg, age sixteen, told the court that policemen had whacked him on the knee in their car after arresting him, and had punched another arrested boy, Harvey Blaustein, seventeen, in the face. Ruttenberg stated that he saw several policemen take Hodas into an anteroom at the station house, where one shouted, "You dirty Jew—," and that screams began, which were then muffled. Dr. Samuel Sandberg, who treated Hodas a few hours later, testified the boy had been terribly beaten, with contusions and welts on his arms and legs. He had to place his arm in a sling. Attorneys, who included Herbert Ehrmann, junior counsel for Sacco and Vanzetti over fifteen years before, declared that the police had made no attempts to chase the Irish American youths, and had not taken down the names of any witnesses.

In the first case involving Irish American-Jewish conflict since the *PM* disclosures, the Irish American judge, Richard Walsh, found guilty the two Jewish boys who were tried as adults and fined them. Jews expressed outrage that, despite many reported acts of antisemitic violence and vandalism in recent months, the police had not made a single arrest. Instead, as *New York Post* columnist Victor Riesel noted, "The first to be found guilty were Jewish lads who attempted to protect themselves." Defense counsel responded to the verdict by asking the judge for a warrant for the arrest of Sergeant Fay on charges of assault and battery for beating Hodas, but the judge refused. The newly-energized Central Advisory Committee of Jewish Organizations vowed to finance an appeal to the U.S. Supreme Court, if necessary. . . .

A Jewish girl in Mattapan on her way to the movies was "set upon" by a group of non-Jewish youths, who told her Jews were no longer going to be allowed to go to movie theaters. The same day, a similar group attacked a Jewish boy in

Roxbury, while a prominent Jewish leader in Dorchester awoke to see swastikas crayoned in front of his house.

Antisemitic beatings escalated in the spring, as warmer weather drew more people outdoors. A gang assaulted two Jewish sixteen-year-olds near Franklin Field in Dorchester, after first asking whether they were Jews. A few days later, twenty Dorchester High School students, at least one of whom wielded a hunting knife and another a club, assaulted three of their Jewish classmates after school on an elevated train. After the beating, one of the Jewish boys had a closed and badly swollen eye. Rabbi Korff stated that he had asked the police that morning to provide protection for Jewish boys at the high school, because Christian students were openly plotting attacks. Teachers had warned the principal that Jewish students were in danger, and he had assigned eight faculty members to patrol the school grounds at closing time. The principal, acting under orders from the school superintendent, refused permission to the three Jewish victims to visit classrooms with the police in order to identify their assailants. Supporters of the victims claimed that the "recent outbreak of attacks" in Dorchester was caused by "a flood of anti-Semitic literature of a particularly virulent nature" that had been "widely circulated in recent weeks."

About two weeks later, seven or eight high school students in Cambridge, a city immediately adjacent to Boston, "badly mauled" two Harvard freshmen walking along the Charles River after demanding to know whether they were Jews. Both victims had to spend the night in the Harvard infirmary. The attack received national attention, although it was almost totally ignored by what *Time* called "Boston's ostrich press." Cambridge's population was 77 percent Irish Catholic, and *Time* described the town as "rife with Coughlinism [and] anti-Semitism."

Similarly in New York, antisemitic violence remained widespread during 1944. *The New York Post* noted that time and again, Jews were being assaulted on the very street corners at which Christian Front and Christian Mobilizers speeches had been given before the war. A fifteen-year-old South Bronx girl who roamed the streets with a "Jew-hunting" band acknowledged in January 1944 that the prewar antisemitic street corner meetings had strongly influenced her. She believed the Christian Front and Christian Mobilizers claims that Jews owned all the wealth and ran the country, and recalled that the streetcorner speakers had told neighborhood residents not to patronize Jewish stores. That month, an antisemitic mob of twenty in a Brooklyn pool hall, shouting "Jew bastard" and "dirty Jews," badly mauled two Jewish teenagers. Although one of the Jews suffered two black eyes from being kicked in the face and stab wounds to his leg, police refused to arrest anyone, dismissing the attack as "just a poolroom fight. . . ."

Several factors contributed to a significant decline in antisemitic violence in Boston and New York after World War II. Public awareness of the horrors of the Holocaust resulted in some diminution of antisemitism. A markedly improved economic climate and better prospects for social mobility reduced frustration and resentment against other groups. The movement of many Jews to suburban neighborhoods lessened direct physical contacts with hostile Irish Americans on the streets. In Boston, the relatively liberal Richard Cushing, whose brother-in-law was Jewish, replaced the archconservative William O'Connell as cardinal in 1944. O'Connell had been uninterested in taking steps to reduce the antisemitic violence, and had not disciplined Christian Front priests. Cushing, by contrast, initiated a considerable amount of interfaith dialogue, and took strong measures in the early 1950s against a reactionary antisemitic movement that had resurfaced in the Boston archdiocese. . . .

The editor of *The Day*, Samuel Margoshes, emphasized that what existed was "a pogrom condition." As in Europe, the youths who carried out the attacks were inspired by virulently antisemitic propaganda, which the Christian Front circulated widely in Boston and New York. They, too, had been influenced by antisemitic views that priests, parents, and other adults propagated in their homes and neighborhoods, and by their diocesan newspapers.

To be sure, government authorities in Boston and New York, unlike many of their European counterparts, did not usually endorse assaults on Jews or attempt to justify them by blaming the Jews for provoking them. In Boston they did, of course, try, convict, and fine two Jewish youths assaulted by an antisemitic crowd, none of whose members were arrested. For the most part, the authorities in both cities claimed that the perpetrators were misguided adolescents lacking parental supervision. William Herlands, New York's Commissioner of Investigation, even reported that the majority of the youths involved in antisemitic beatings and vandalism were "mentally retarded or sexually perverted." Yet, as in European pogroms, many policemen sympathized with the marauding antisemitic bands, refused to arrest the attackers, and even sometimes themselves delighted in physically abusing innocent Jewish youths. High government officials, including police commissioners and mayors in both cities, and even the governor of Massachusetts for a considerable length of time, remained indifferent to severe outbreaks of antisemitism, taking little or no action against them.

Youth Antiwar Rebellion

Charles Phillips

Throughout the late 1960s and into the early 70s, the United States had become divided over the conflict in Vietnam. Thousands of young Americans had been killed fighting in a war that many believed could not be won. After being elected in 1969, President Richard Nixon pledged to begin withdrawing troops from the country. However, because of the Veit Cong's use of sanctuaries in a neutral country, Nixon chose to expand U.S. involvement in the war in 1970. Young people across the country were outraged. Overnight, college campuses were transformed into political battle grounds. Protests and sit-ins were swiftly organized. Students at Kent State University in Ohio arranged a weekend of anti-war events followed by a Monday-afternoon rally in objection to Nixon's decision. But what was supposed to be a nonviolent show of dissent quickly erupted into mayhem. While police tried to keep order on Friday and Saturday, students smashed windows of area businesses and burned a campus building to the ground. Monday's peaceful protest escalated into thirteen seconds of violent confusion that left nine students injured and four dead. In the following article, author Charles Phillips relates the events leading up to that tragic day and the aftermath of its violence. Phillips has contributed articles to American History *magazine.*

One spring day on a grassy hillside better suited for blankets and young lovers, a spiraling madness propelled by events far away came crashing down on Kent, Ohio. On May 4, 1970, a 13-second spasm of violence on the Kent State University Commons left four students dead and nine wounded, and exposed to the world the extent to which the Vietnam War had divided Americans.

Charles Phillips, "A Day to Remember: May 4, 1970," *American History*, vol. 39, iss. 2, June 2004, pp. 16–19. Reproduced by permission.

A Nation Divided

The number of U.S. troops fighting in Vietnam climbed during the John F. Kennedy and Lyndon B. Johnson administrations. By the late 1960s, Johnson's visionary programs to end poverty and inequality in America collapsed as the required dollars were diverted to the war, where thousands of young Americans were dying in a conflict few in the nation understood. Hundreds of thousands of Vietnamese civilians also suffered and died, their homes destroyed by napalm, defoliants and bombs, their society torn asunder. The war was likewise tearing at America's soul, as much of the world decried "American imperialism."

By 1967 Americans were seriously divided by the Vietnam War. The country seemed headed for open rebellion. Many feared that our goals in Southeast Asia were at least hopeless, if not morally wrong. America's college campuses became the centers for opposition, and an unyielding LBJ was the main target. Faced with growing protests and the demoralizing North Vietnamese Tet Offensive of early 1968, as well as serious challenges to his presidency from Democratic Senators Eugene McCarthy and Robert Kennedy, Johnson shocked the nation on March 31 by announcing a peace initiative with North Vietnam and stating that he would not seek reelection.

Shock followed shock in 1968. Urban riots came on the heels of Martin Luther King's murder in April. Robert Kennedy was assassinated on June 5. In August authorities and antiwar protestors violently clashed during the Democratic convention in Chicago, where Hubert H. Humphrey won the party's nomination for president.

After a campaign supporting some of LBJ's much-vilified policies, Humphrey was narrowly defeated in November by Republican Richard M. Nixon, who had touted a law-and-order platform and a "secret plan" to end the war.

President Nixon's plan was to turn the fighting over to the South Vietnamese army and begin withdrawing American troops. Frustrated by the Viet Cong use of sanctuaries in neutral Cambodia, however, Nixon ordered a series of secret bombings of the VC operations there in early 1970. Because the airstrikes proved ineffectual, on April 30, 1970. Nixon—who had pledged to end the war—announced a U.S. ground incursion into Cambodia that expanded the war.

The next day, Friday, May 1, students protested across the country. At Kent State University, a few hundred students, in a mock funeral, buried a copy of the Constitution, claiming it had been murdered when U.S. troops were sent into Cambodia without a congressional declaration of war. Plans for a Monday antiwar rally were announced.

From Bad to Worse

That night, after police attempted an early closing of bars overflowing with angry students, the two groups clashed in downtown Kent, and students smashed storefront windows as they were driven back to campus. The following day the city imposed a dusk-to-dawn curfew and requested the National Guard be sent to Kent. Students, confined to the campus, organized an antiwar protest, and some 2,000 students joined in. They converged after dark on the World War II-era wooden building on the fringe of the Commons that housed the Reserve Officer Training Corps (ROTC). Soon the structure was engulfed in flames, with students cutting the hoses of firemen sent to the scene. As the building burned that night, National Guard troops sent by Ohio Governor James A. Rhodes rolled onto campus, clearing students from the Commons.

On Sunday, May 3, the Republican governor arrived in town, promising to use "every force possible" to maintain order and drive the protesters out of Kent. He called them "worse than the brown shirts and the communist element, and also the nightriders and the vigilantes. They are the worst type of people we harbor in America."

On campus it was a tense but quiet Sunday until that night, when students again marched on campus, eventually blocking Main Street at the campus gate. Their demand now was "pigs off campus," since to the students the Guard had come to embody the war and its leaders. After negotiations between city and university officials broke down, Guard and state police helicopters circled as the protesters were driven back with tear gas, batons and bayonets. Many were chased down and beaten, pursued into dormitories and even the library. As many middle-of-the-road students watched this action, they were angered and radicalized.

When classes resumed Monday morning, debate about recent events and what was to come displaced academics. Although the Guard apparently controlled the campus, many students decided to attend the previously called-for noon rally. At 11 a.m. they began to gather on the Commons, and by noon the crowd had swelled to an estimated 3,000. Acting on a decision made earlier, a Kent State policeman began ordering the students to disperse. Until then the assembly had been peaceful and orderly, but the dispersal order incited the crowd, which responded with chants, jeers and some rock throwing.

The Boiling Point

Donning gas masks, about 100 guardsmen began firing tear gas into the crowd. Three units were ordered to disperse the crowd by advancing across the Commons, driving the students up and over a knoll known as Blanket Hill and then down into a parking lot and football practice field. After several minutes spent lobbing tear gas canisters at students, who often defiantly hurled them back, Troop G retraced its steps back up Blanket Hill toward the Commons. Suddenly, at the crest of the hill, with students following and taunting the troops, 28 guardsmen wheeled and fired on students. At 12:25 p.m., 61 shots from M-1 rifles and .45-caliber pistols rained down the hill for 13 seconds.

The nearest casualty was 20 yards from the Guard, the farthest 250 yards. Four students—Allison Krause, Jeffrey Miller, Sandra Scheuer and William Schroeder—lay dead in the parking lot, and nine others were wounded. As the stunned crowd tried to comprehend what had just happened and rushed to aid the wounded, the Guard marched back across the Commons.

Many of the students, horrified and enraged, reassembled facing the regrouped guardsmen. Fearing further bloodshed, faculty marshals begged the Guard to refrain from any provocative actions and allow them time to convince the angry, distraught students to disperse to avoid another confrontation. By 1:30 they had succeeded, and the students began to leave. With the Guard at parade rest around the remains of the ROTC building, the university was closed indefinitely and, like the 20,000 students ordered to vacate the campus, a shock wave of reaction to the violence began spreading from Blanket Hill across the nation and the world.

The Aftermath

During the next five days, more than 500 American colleges and universities were closed. By mid-May, some 5 million students had joined the national student antiwar strike. During that same fortnight, fires raged as students torched 30 ROTC buildings, and the University of Wisconsin alone reported 27 firebombings. May 1970 became the month with the most arson incidents since the government began keeping such statistics.

On May 9, 1970, more than 150,000 protesters converged on Washington, D.C., where President Nixon huddled in a White House protected by armed military guards and surrounded by a cordon of bumper-to-bumper buses. The "bunker mentality" that characterized Nixon's presidency was never more evident.

On May 15, police killed two students during protests at Jackson State University in Mississippi. On Armed Forces Day, May 16, some 43 antiwar veterans groups held marches, rallies and music festivals at 22 U.S. military bases, and military leaders canceled Armed Forces Day events at 28 other bases because antiwar demonstrations were planned. More than 900 colleges and universities—some 80 percent of academia— closed before the end of May 1970 due to protests. Some 175,000 faculty members nationwide had joined the students, and more than 35,000 national guardsmen in 16 states had been called into action. The protests did not stop with the campuses. After the Kent killings, there were reports of entire companies of U.S. troops in Vietnam refusing orders to invade Cambodia. In displays of solidarity with the students, numerous American soldiers wore black armbands and objected to fighting any longer in Vietnam.

The Search for Justice

Back in Kent, the FBI and state police conducted investigations. In addition, a special state grand jury was convened to investigate the events, ultimately exonerating the guardsmen but indicting 25 people, most of them students, for offenses that occurred on campus before the shootings. On May 24, President Nixon appointed a high-level commission to study the violence at Kent and campuses around the country.

The President's Commission on Campus Unrest reported its findings on September 26, dividing responsibility for the events of May 4. "The actions of some students were violent and criminal and those of some others were dangerous, reckless, and irresponsible," said the report. The commission's findings of Guard responsibility were more damning: "The rally was peaceful and there was no apparent impending violence. Only when the guard attempted to disperse the rally did some students react violently. . . . The indiscriminant firing of rifles into a crowd of students and the deaths that followed were unnecessary, unwarranted, and inexcusable. . . . Even if the guardsmen faced danger, it was not a danger which called for lethal force. The 61 shots fired by 28 guardsmen certainly cannot be justified."

The courtroom battles—state and federal, criminal and civil—over Kent State continued for years and included a landmark 1974 U.S. Supreme Court ruling, Scheuer v. Rhodes, which profoundly weakened the long-standing doctrine of sovereign immunity. Yet, no guardsmen were ever found criminally responsible for the killings.

Long after the war and the chants of student protest ended, the search for justice by the families and supporters of the 13 victims at Kent continued. Finally, nearly a decade after the event, the state of Ohio settled a civil suit on January 4, 1979, that included a $650,000 cash settlement for the victims and their families and an official "statement of regret" signed by 28 defendants.

The War at Home

Vietnam was the first televised war, reaching the American public in a series of dramatic and disturbing images. At Kent State, the unforgettable photo of a bewildered and grief-stricken young woman kneeling beside the body of the slain Jeffrey Miller seemed to capture the tragedy of the time when a war half a world away came home to the streets of America.

An Increase in Broken and Single-Parent Households May Lead to Youth Violence

Patrick F. Fagan

Researchers, politicians, and social scientists have been conducting studies for decades, trying to find the root causes of violence among young people. While many have pointed to poverty, race relations, or violent images in the media as major contributing factors, others feel that many people are ignoring a key element in the cycle of violence: the breakdown of the American family. Author Patrick F. Fagan argues that an increase in the number of single-parent households during the last decades of the twentieth century and into the new millennium is the real reason for violence among today's youth. Fagan asserts that many children from broken and single-parent households lack positive role models and a stable home environment. The author feels that these factors make them far more likely to become involved in criminal activities as young adults. When these youths have their own children, they pass their destructive behavior patterns down to their sons and daughters, perpetuating the cycle of violence and crime. Fagan is a William H.G. FitzGerald Research Fellow in Family and Cultural Issues for The Heritage Foundation.

A Never-Ending Cycle

Broken or dysfunctional homes are the main factors in determining if a child will grow up to be violent. Without the proper parental role models, a child will grow up in an atmosphere devoid of love or empathy. The social evolution of a criminal occurs in several stages. First, he is born into a highly unstable home atmosphere. Most violent criminals were raised

Patrick F. Fagan, "Disintegration of the Family is the Real Root Cause of Violent Crime," *USA Today Magazine*, May 1996. Copyright © 1996 Society for the Advancement of Education. Reproduced by permission.

in dysfunctional families, in an atmosphere of drugs, crime, and domestic violence. This causes him to have trouble in school and he becomes a behavioral problem. He begins to socialize with others like him, eventually joining a gang and committing crimes such as burglary and vandalism. During stage four he begins to commit violent crimes. Finally, he gets his girlfriend pregnant and the cycle starts over. Children growing up under these influences are virtually assured of perpetuating the destructive cycle.

Social scientists, criminologists, and many other observers at long last are coming to recognize the connection between the breakdown of families and various social problems that have plagued American society. In the debate over welfare reform, for instance, it now is a widely accepted premise that children born into single-parent families are much more likely than those in intact families to fall into poverty and welfare dependency.

While the link between the family and chronic welfare dependency is understood much better these days, there is another link—between the family and crime—that deserves more attention. Entire communities, particularly in urban areas, are being torn apart by crime. We desperately need to uncover the real root cause of criminal behavior and learn how criminals are formed in order to be able to fight this situation.

There is a wealth of evidence in the professional literature of criminology and sociology to suggest that the breakdown of family is the real root cause of crime in the U.S. Yet, the orthodox thinking in official Washington assumes that it is caused by material conditions, such as poor employment opportunities and a shortage of adequately funded state and Federal social programs. . . .

The Wrong Focus

Still, Federal bureaucrats and lawmakers persist in arguing that poverty is the primary cause of crime. In its simplest form, this contention is absurd; if it were true, there would have been more crime in the past, when more people were poorer. Moreover, in less-developed nations, the crime rates would be higher than in the U.S. History defies the assumption that deteriorating economic circumstances breed crime and improving conditions reduce it. America's crime rate actually rose during the long period of economic growth in the early 20th century. As the Great Depression set in and incomes dropped, the crime rate also fell. It went up again between 1965 and 1974, when incomes rose. Most recently, during the recession of 1982, there was a slight dip in crime, not an increase.

Washington also believes that race is the second most important cause of crime. The large disparity in crime rates between whites and blacks often is cited as proof. However, a closer look at the data shows that the real variable is not race, but family structure and all that it implies in terms of commitment and love between adults and children. . . .

The Evolution of a Criminal

There is a strong, well-documented pattern of circumstances and social evolution in the life of a future violent criminal. The pattern may be summarized in five basic stages:

Stage one: Parental neglect and abandonment of the child in early home life. When the future violent criminal is born, his father already has abandoned the mother. If his parents are married, they are likely to divorce by the third year of his life. He is raised in a neighborhood with a high concentration of single-parent families. He does not become securely attached to his mother during the critical early years. His child care frequently changes.

The adults in his life often quarrel and vent their frustrations physically. He, or a member of his family, may suffer one or more forms of abuse, including sexual. There is much harshness in his home, and he is deprived of affection.

He becomes hostile, anxious, and hyperactive. He is difficult to manage at age three and is labeled a "behavior problem." Lacking his father's presence and attention, he becomes increasingly aggressive.

Stage two: The embryonic gang becomes a place for him to belong. His behavior continues to deteriorate at a rapid rate. He satisfies his needs by exploiting others. At age five or six, he hits his mother. In first grade, his aggressive behavior causes problems for other children. He is difficult for school officials to handle.

He is rejected socially at school by "normal" children. He searches for and finds acceptance among similarly aggressive and hostile youngsters. He and his friends are slower at school. They fail at verbal tasks that demand abstract thinking and at learning social and moral concepts. His reading scores trail behind the rest of his class. He has lessening interest in school, teachers, and learning.

By now, he and his friends have low educational and life expectations for themselves. These are reinforced by teachers and family members. Poor supervision at home continues. His father, or father substitute, still is absent. His life primarily is characterized by aggressive behavior by himself and his peers and a hostile home life.

Stage three: He joins a delinquent gang. At age 11, his bad habits and attitudes are well-established. By age 15, he engages in criminal behavior. The earlier he commits his first delinquent act, the longer he will be likely to lead a life of crime.

His companions are the main source of his personal identity and his sense of belonging. Life with his delinquent friends is hidden from adults. The number of delinquent acts increases in the year before he and his friends drop out of school.

His delinquent girlfriends have poor relationships with their mothers, as well as with "normal" girls in school. A number of his peers use drugs. Many, especially the girls, run away from home or just drift away.

Stage four: He commits violent crime and the full-fledged criminal gang emerges. High violence grows in his community with the increase in the number of single-parent families. He purchases a gun, at first mainly for self-defense. He and his peers begin to use violence for exploitation. The violent young men in his delinquent peer group are arrested more than the nonviolent criminals, but most of them do not get caught at all.

Gradually, different friends specialize in different types of crime—violence or theft. Some are more versatile than others. The girls are involved in prostitution, while he and the other boys are members of criminal gangs.

Stage five: A new child—and a new generation of criminals—is born. His 16-year-old girlfriend is pregnant. He has no thought of marrying her; among his peers this simply isn't done. They stay together for awhile until the shouting and hitting start. He leaves her and does not see the baby anymore.

One or two of his criminal friends are experts in their field. Only a few members of the group to which he now belongs—career criminals—are caught. They commit hundreds of crimes per year. Most of those he and his friends commit are in their own neighborhood.

For the future violent criminal, each of these five stages is characterized by the absence of the love, affection, and dedication of his parents. The ordinary tasks of growing up are a series of perverse exercises, frustrating his needs, stunting his capacity for empathy as well as his ability to belong, and increasing the risk of his becoming a twisted young adult. This experience is in stark contrast to the investment of love and dedication by two parents normally needed to make compassionate, competent adults out of their offspring.

The Impact of Violent Crime

When one considers some of the alarming statistics that make headlines today, the future of our society appears bleak. In the mid 1980s, the chancellor of the New York City school system warned: "We are in a situation now where 12,000 of our 60,000 kindergartners have mothers who are still in their teenage years and where 40% of our students come from single-parent households."

Today, this crisis is not confined to New York; it afflicts even small, rural communities. Worse yet, the national illegitimacy rate is predicted to reach 50% within the next 12–20 years. As a result, violence in school is becoming worse. The Centers for Disease Control recently reported that more than four percent of high school students surveyed had brought a firearm at least once to school. Many of them, in fact, were regular gun carriers.

The old injunction clearly is true—violence begets violence. Violent families are producing violent youths, and violent youths are producing violent communities. The future violent criminal is likely to have witnessed numerous conflicts between his parents. He may have been physically or sexually abused. His parents, brothers, and sisters also may be criminals, and thus his family may have a disproportionate negative impact on the community. Moreover, British and American studies show that fewer than five percent of all criminals account for 50% of all criminal convictions. Over all, there has been an extraordinary increase in community violence in most major American cities.

Government agencies are powerless to make men and women marry or stay wed. They are powerless to guarantee that parents will love and care for their children. They are powerless to persuade anyone to make and keep promises. In fact, government agencies often do more harm than good by enforcing policies that undermine stable families and by misdiagnosing the real root cause of such social problems as violent crime.

Nevertheless, ordinary Americans are not powerless. They know full well how to fight crime effectively. They do not need to survey the current social science literature to know that a family life of affection, cohesion, and parental involvement prevents delinquency, They instinctively realize that paternal and maternal affection and the father's presence in the home are among the critical elements in raising well-balanced children. They acknowledge that parents should encourage the moral development of their offspring—an act that best is accomplished within the context of religious belief and practice.

None of this is to say that fighting crime or rebuilding stable families and communities will be easy. What is easy is deciding what we must do at the outset. Begin by affirming four simple principles: First, marriage is vital. Second, parents must love and nurture their children in spiritual as well as physical ways. Third, children must be taught how to relate to and empathize with others. Finally, the backbone of strong neighborhoods and communities is friendship and cooperation among families.

These principles constitute the real root solution to the problem of violent crime. We should do everything in our power to apply them in our own lives and the life of the nation, not just for our sake, but for that of our children.

Gun Availability Contributes to Youth Violence

Randy M. Page and Jon Hammermeister

The number of violent crimes committed with a weapon has exploded in the last several decades. Gun control is an issue of much debate in the United States. Some people feel that strict legislation would violate the rights of people that obtain firearms legally. Others believe that firmer laws are the only way to reduce the number of violent crimes, especially among youthful offenders. In the following selection, Jon Hammermeister and Randy M. Page argue that government intervention is needed to help make the country's streets and schools safer. For this article, the two gathered the results of extensive testing that suggests that the availability of weapons is a primary enabler of violent crime among youths. These results show that guns, both stolen from homes and purchased on the street, are the weapon of choice among students regardless of gender, race, or location. The authors outline a plan for the government to unite together with schools and communities across the nation to reduce the number of weapons that fall into the hands of potentially violent youths. Hammermeister is a college instructor and Page works as a journalist.

Many studies have demonstrated that the availability of guns is responsible for the rise in violence among juveniles. These studies indicate that more than one-third of urban high school students have easy access to a gun, and many teens have access to a firearm in their own homes. Four out of every five guns brought to school come from the students' homes, and handgun ownership among inner-city high-school youths is closely associated with delinquent behavior. A substantial number of murders and suicides among teenagers involve firearms. Tighter gun control laws are needed to control the spread of firearm-related youth violence.

A higher incidence of weapon-carrying, guns in particular, among youths has been identified as a key factor in the recent increase in youth violence. Weapon-carrying increases risk of death and serious injury to both the carrier and others. In recent years a number of studies have investigated the accessibility of weapons and the extent to which youth carry them.

Weapons Are Common Among Students

According to the 1990 Youth Risk Behavior Survey, 1 in 20 senior high school students carried a firearm, usually a handgun, and 1 in 5 carried a weapon of some type during the 30 days preceding the survey (Centers for Diseases Control, 1991). A survey of 10 inner-city high schools in four states found that 35 percent of male and 11 percent of female students reported carrying a gun (Sheley, McGee, & Wright, 1992). A study of rural school students in southeast Texas found that 6 percent of male students had taken guns to school, and almost 2 percent reported that they did so almost every day. In addition, 42.3 percent of those surveyed said they could get a gun if they wanted one (Kissell, 1993). More than one-third (34 percent) of urban high school students in Seattle reported having easy access to handguns, while 11.4 percent of males and 1.5 percent of females reported owning a handgun. One-third of those who owned handguns reported that they had fired at someone. Further, almost 10 percent of female students reported a firearm homicide or suicide among family members or close friends (Callahan & Rivara, 1992). Another study from the southeast U.S. found that 9 percent of urban and suburban youth owned a handgun (Larson, 1994).

A poll of students in grades six through twelve conducted by Louis Harris for the Harvard School of Public Health in 1993 found that 59 percent said they could get a handgun if they wanted one, and 21 percent said they could get one within the hour. More than 60 percent of urban youth reported that they could get a handgun, and 58 percent of suburban youth also claimed that they could (Larson, 1994). Fifteen percent of students reported carrying a handgun in the past month, 11 percent said that they had been shot at, 9 percent said that they had fired a gun at someone, and 4 percent said they had carried a gun to school in the past year (Drevitch, 1994; Hull, 1993).

In a study of two public inner-city junior high schools in Washington, D.C., 47 percent of males reported having ever carried knives, and 25 percent reported having ever carried guns for protection or to use in case they got into a fight; 37 percent of females reported having carried a knife for these purposes. Both schools are located in high-crime areas (Webster, Gainer, & Champion, 1993).

Reason for Gun Possession

A common reason given by young people for carrying weapons is for protection against being "jumped" (Price, Desmond, & Smith, 1991). However, research has shown that weapon-carrying among youth appears to be more closely associated with criminal activity, delinquency, and aggressiveness than to purely defensive behavior (Sheley, McGee, & Wright, 1992; Webster, Gainer, & Champion, 1993). Handgun ownership by inner-city high school youth has been associated with gang membership, selling drugs, interpersonal violence, being convicted of crimes, and either suspension or expulsion from school (Callahan & Rivara, 1992). Gun-carrying among junior-high students is also strongly linked with indicators of serious delinquency, such as having been arrested (Webster, Gainer, & Champion, 1993). These studies have the following implications for the prevention of gun-carrying among youth (Webster, Gainer, & Champion, 1993).

If gun carrying stems largely from antisocial attitudes and behaviors rather than from purely defensive motives of otherwise nonviolent youths, interventions designed to prevent delinquency may be more effective than those that focus only on educating youths about the risks associated with carrying a gun. The latter may, however, be able to deter less hardened youths from carrying weapons in the future. Intensive and comprehensive interventions directed at high-risk children could possibly "inoculate" children against the many social factors that foster criminal deviance and the most violent behavior patterns.

How Youths Get Guns

Adult criminals and youth involved in illegal activities have reported that guns are not difficult to obtain. Illegal or unregulated transactions are the primary sources of guns used in violent acts; stealing, borrowing from friends or acquaintances, and illegal purchasing of guns are the most common. Less than 1 in 5 guns used for illegal activities were purchased from licensed dealers. The most commonly cited reason for acquiring a gun is "self-defense." (Roth, 1994).

Every day in the United States there are 733 shootings (Cotton, 1992). It is estimated that 66.7 million handguns and 200 million firearms of all kinds are in circulation (Larson, 1994). About one-half of all households own at least one firearm and one-quarter own a handgun (Reiss & Roth, 1993). Experts assert that greater availability of guns increases the rates of murder and felony gun use. However, the greater availability of guns does not appear to affect levels of violence in general (Roth, 1994). . . .

Firearm Violence and Youth

Among teenagers 15 to 19 years of age and young adults 20 to 24 years of age, 1 of every 4 deaths is by a firearm. One of every 8 deaths in children 10 to 14 is by a firearm. For those 15 to 19 there are substantial variations by race and sex in the percentage of deaths due to firearms. Among African-American teenage males, 60 percent of deaths result from firearm injury compared with 23 percent of white teenage males. Among African-American teenage females it is 22 percent compared with 10 percent of white female teenagers (Fingerhut, 1993). The number of African-American males aged 15 to 19 who died from gunshot wounds in 1990 was nearly five times higher than the number who died from AIDS, sickle-cell disease, and all other natural causes combined. (Fingerhut, 1993; Kellerman, 1994).

In 1990, 82 percent of all homicide victims aged 15 to 19 (91 percent and 77 percent African-American and white males, respectively) and 76 percent of victims aged 20 to 24 (87 percent and 71 percent among African-American and white males, respectively) were killed with guns. Firearm homicide for African-American males 15 to 19 years of age was 11 times the rate among white males, 105.3 compared with 9.7 per 100,000 population. The rate for African-American females was five times the rate for white females, 10.4 compared with 2.0 per 100,000 population (Fingerhut, 1993).

In 1990, 67.3 percent of all suicides among teenagers aged 15 to 19 were the result of firearms. Since 1985 the overall rate of suicide for teenagers by firearms increased from 6.0 to 7.5 per 100,000. The group of teenagers with the largest percent increase was African-American males; however, white male teenagers (13.5 per 100,000) had a higher firearm suicide rate in 1990 compared with African-American males (8.8 per 100,000). During this same time period, the rate of suicide not involving firearms decreased for both African-American and white males and females (Fingerhut, 1993).

Crackdown on Weapons in Schools

Schools are grappling with the problem of protecting children and school staff from the violence surrounding them. Episodes of violence, particularly gun violence, are increasing in schools (Nordland, 1992) and violent attacks involving even elementary school children appear to be on the increase. Thus, gun violence has become a major concern for schools across the nation—a concern that is no longer limited to large cities, but extends to smaller cities and rural areas (Morganthau, 1992).

School security and law enforcement officials estimate that four of every five firearms that are carried into schools come from the students' homes; they bring one of their parents' firearms for "show and tell" with friends. Law enforcement officials also note that firearms are easily accessible by other means. They are readily borrowed from friends, bought by proxy, stolen, or even rented. On the street, guns can be purchased for as little as 25 dollars.

The following position paper of the National Association of Secondary School Principals Board on Weapons in Schools outlines the need to control weapons and offers several ways in which educators can work toward that end (Kressly, 1994).

Whereas, students have a right to attend school without a fear of weapons' violence to themselves or others;

Whereas, safe schools enhance the learning environment, necessary to quality schools, which are essential to a successful democracy;

Whereas, the causes of violence are multiple: chronic poverty, the lack of jobs and role models, the disintegration of families, the loss of moral values, and a popular culture that seems to glorify violence at every turn;

Whereas, a major 1993 Louis Harris poll about guns among American youth reports that 1 in 25 students takes a handgun to school in a single month, and 59 percent know where to get a handgun if they need one;

Whereas, violence is exacerbated with the increase of weapons in our schools, resulting in some 31 deaths from guns during the 1992-93 school year; be it therefore known that the National Association of Secondary School Principals:

- supports passage of the Brady Bill, which requires a waiting period and background check before legal purchase of a handgun;

- urges full enforcement of the Gun-Free School Zones Act of 1990;

- calls on Congress to pass the Safe Schools Act of 1993, with an amendment that will ban the purchase of a handgun and semi-automatic guns for any person under the age of 21;

- urges schools to provide staff training for weapons situations arising in school, and to implement student awareness programs which challenge youths' falsely held beliefs that they are invincible;

- challenges schools to implement apprehension, prevention, intervention, and counseling programs to combat possession of weapons and violent acts;

- encourages school-based parent involvement programs to include violence prevention strategies that emphasize the issue of easy access to handguns;

- exhorts school districts to establish violence prevention curriculum, grades K-12, and promote articulation among levels to ensure continuity in policies and practices;

- challenges Schools of Education to add conflict resolution and violence coping skills to their teacher preparation programs.

Controlling the Epidemic

When weapons are carried into schools, especially guns, the potential for a violent episode is heightened and, in recent years, there have been far too many violent episodes involving weapons on school campuses that have led to tragedy (Morganthau, 1992). Preventing violence calls for school policies that provide for school environments that are free from violence for students, staff, and others on school premises (Friedlander, 1993). For some school systems this may mean providing such controls as locker searches, weapons searches, hiring police to patrol school premises, allowing students to wear only see-through backpacks, and possibly providing metal detectors upon entry. Some school systems have even created separate alternative schools for young people with a history of violent and abusive behavior. While this option is attracting attention, it is also controversial (Harrington-Lueker, 1992).

A study by the American School Board revealed that 50 percent of school districts conduct locker searches, 36 percent conduct search and seizure activities, 36 percent maintain security personnel in schools, 31 percent have gun-free school zones, and 15 percent have metal detectors (Natale, 1994). Approximately one-fourth of large urban school districts in the United States use metal detectors to help reduce weapon-carrying in schools (Centers for Disease Control, 1993). According to the Centers for Disease Control, these detectors may help reduce, but do not eliminate, weapon-carrying in schools and to and from schools. Students who attended schools with metal detector programs were as likely as those attending schools without metal detectors to carry weapons elsewhere, but were less likely to have carried a weapon inside the school building (7.8 percent versus 13.6 percent) or going to and from school (7.7 percent versus 15.2 percent). Decreases in school-related weapon-carrying were due to decreases in the carrying of both knives and handguns. The presence of metal detectors had no apparent effect on the prevalence of threats and physical fights inside the school, to and from school, or anywhere else (Centers for Disease Control, 1993).

Security measures and equipment are expensive; walk-through metal detectors can cost up to $10,000 each and X-ray equipment designed to detect weapons in book bags can cost as much as $17,000. Hiring security personnel is also expensive. Despite these measures, students are known to have successfully carried weapons into schools, usually by sneaking them through windows or unguarded entrances, much to the frustration of many school administrators. Some school districts arc reluctant to implement new security measures, particularly metal detectors, because they fear it may open them up to lawsuits (Glazer, 1992).

The Need for Cooperative Action

It is obvious that schools alone cannot be totally effective in controlling availability of weapons. Controlling access will require the cooperation of many individuals and institutions. The New York Academy of Medicine (1994) has proposed the following:

1. Implementing a national licensure system for firearm possession;
2. Limiting the manufacture, sale, and distribution of military-style assault weapons;
3. Increasing the tax on firearms and ammunition;
4. Tightening federal licensing requirements for gun dealers;
5. Limiting the number of guns an individual can buy;
6. Implementing a gun return program;
7. Implementing a firearm fatality and injury reporting system; and
8. Educating the public to the dangers of guns and the need for national regulation.

Sources Cited

- Centers for Disease Control. (1991). Weapon-carrying among high school students—United States, 1990. *Morbidity and Mortality Weekly Report*, 40, 681–684.

- Centers for Disease Control. (1993). Violence-related attitudes and behaviors of high school students—New York City, 1992. *Morbidity and Mortality Weekly Report*, 42, 773–777.

- Centers for Disease Control. (1994). Deaths resulting from firearm- and motor vehicle-related injuries— United States, 1968–1991. *Morbidity and Mortality Weekly Report*, 43, 37–42.

- Cotton, P. (1992). Gun-associated violence increasingly viewed as public health challenge. *Journal of the American Medical Association*, 267, 1171–1173.

- Drevitch, G. (1994). River of blood, river of tears. *Scholastic Update*, February 11, 4–5

- Fingerhut, L.A. (1993). Firearm mortality among children, youth, and young adults 1–34 years of age, trends and current status: United States, 1985–90. *Advance Data from Vital and Health Statistics* (No. 231). Hyattsville, MD: National Center for Health Statistics.

- Fingerhut, L.A., Jones, C., & Makuc, D.M. (1994). Firearm and motor vehicle injury mortality—Variations by state, race, and ethnicity: United States, 1990–1991. *Advance Data from Vital and Health Statistics* (No. 242). Hyattsville, MD: National Center for Health Statistics.

- Friedlander, B.Z. (1993). We can fight violence in the schools. *Educational Digest*, May, 11–14.

- Glazer, S. (1992). Violence in schools. *CQ Researcher*, September 11, 787–803.

- Harrington-Lueker, D. (1992). Blown away by school violence. *American School Board Journal*, 179, 20–26.

- Hull, J.D. (1993). A boy and a gun: Even in a town like Omaha, Nebraska, the young are packing weapons in a deadly battle against fear and boredom. *Time*, August 2, 21–27.

- Kellerman, A.L. (1994). Annotation: Firearm-related violence—What we don't know is killing us. *American Journal of Public Health*, 84, 541–542.

- Kissell, K.P. (1993). Guns on rise in rural schools. *The Morning Call*, March 21.

- Kressly, J.C. (1994). Targeting potential violence before tragedy strikes. *Schools in the Middle*, February, 27–30.

- Larson, E. (1994). *Lethal passage: How the travels of a single handgun expose the roots of America's gun crisis.* New York: Crown.

- Morganthau, T. (1992). It's not just New York . . . Big cities, small towns: More and more guns in younger hands. *Newsweek*, March 9, 25–29.

- Natale, J.A. (1994). Roots of violence. *American School Board Journal*, March, 33–40.

- New York Academy of Medicine. (1994). Firearm violence and public health: Limiting the availability of guns. *Journal of the American Medical Association*, 271, 1281–1283.

- Nordland, R. (1992). Deadly lessons. *Newsweek*, March 9, 22–24.

- Price, J.H., Desmond, S.M., & Smith, D. (1991). Inner city adolescents' perceptions of guns—A preliminary investigation. *Journal of School Health*, 61, 255–259.

- Reiss, A.J., & Roth, J.A. (1993). *Understanding and preventing violence: Panel on the understanding and control of violent behavior.* Washington, D.C.: National Academy Press.

- Roth, J.A. (1994). Firearms and violence. *National Institute of Justice: Research in Brief,* February, 1–7.

- Sheley, J.F., McGee, Z.T., & Wright, J.D. (1992). Gun-related violence in and around inner-city schools. *American Journal of Diseases in Children,* 146, 677–682.

- Webster, D.W., Gainer, P.S., & Champion, H.R. (1993). Weapon carrying among inner-city junior high school students: Defensive behavior vs. aggressive delinquency. *American Journal of Public Health,* 83, 1604–1608.

Poverty Breeds Violence

Mike Males

During the mid to late 1990s, the rate of violent crimes among youths seemed to reach its boiling point. The media focus on youth gangs and school shootings portrayed young people as out of control with little hope of being helped. People soon started to look for somewhere to place the blame. The surge in juvenile delinquents was attributed to everything from TV, to video games, to rap music. In the following selection, Mike Males argues that the real root of the problem of teenage delinquency isn't violent images flickering to life on our nation's television and movie screens, but rather a matter of simple economics. Males points to an increasing number of children and young people living at or below the poverty level as the true cause of youth violence. The author explains that unstable living situations often breed crime and violence among young people. Males asserts that stopping youth violence has to start with reducing child poverty. Males is a professor of sociology at the University of California, Santa Cruz.

In previous decades, American politicians and social scientists predicted waves of violence stemming from "impulsive" blacks, volatile Eastern European immigrants, "hot-blooded" Latin Americans, and other groups "scientifically" judged to harbor innately aggressive traits. In each case, the news media joined in vilifying whatever temporarily unpopular minority that politicians and pseudo-science had flocked to blame.

And in each case, the branding of disfavored population groups as inherently violent has been disproven. (See Stephen

Mike Males, "Wild in Deceit: Why 'Teen Violence' is Poverty Violence in Disguise," *Extra!* March-April, 1996. Reproduced by permission of Fairness and Accuracy in Reporting.

Jay Gould's *The Mismeasure of Man* for examples.) In each case, violence has been found to be a straightforward function of poverty, income disparity.

Here we go again.

Experts have identified a 1990s demographic scapegoat for America's pandemic violent crime: our own kids. A mushrooming media scare campaign about the coming "storm" of "teenage violence" waged by liberal and conservative politicians and experts alike is in full roar.

Teenage Time Bombs

Blaming "a ticking demographic time bomb," *U.S. News & World Report* (12/4/95) warns of "scary kids around the corner." The "troublesome demographic trends" are a growing adolescent population.

"A Teenage Time Bomb," *Time* announced (1/15/96), quoting Northeastern University criminologist James Alan Fox's view of teenagers as "temporary sociopaths—impulsive and immature." Added *Time*: "If [teens] also have easy access to guns and drugs, they can be extremely dangerous."

Other top-quoted criminologists, like University of California, Los Angeles's James Q. Wilson and former American Society of Criminology president Alfred Blumstein, are in full agreement with Fox: Young equals violent. And top political officials concur. The *Los Angeles Times* (12/18/95) noted Federal Bureau of Investigations Director Louis Freeh and other authorities' alarm over "the fact that the crime-prone 16-to-24 year-old group will grow dramatically over the next decade— which Freeh cited as 'an alarming indicator of future trends.'"

The trendiest demographic scapegoater is the centrist Brookings Institution's John DiIulio Jr., anointed "The Crime Doctor" and "one of Washington's in-vogue thinkers" by the *L.A. Times* (5/2/95). "More male teenagers, more crime. Period," is his message. A new breed of youthful "superpredators" menace the nation, so vicious even hardened adult convicts are scared of them, DiIulio said.

Journalists ought to be aware they are pouring gasoline on a fire they have already fanned. A 1994 Gallup Poll (*Gallup Poll Monthly*, 9/94) found that American adults already hold "a greatly inflated view of the amount of crime committed by people under the age of 18," with the most salient reason "news coverage of violent crime committed by juveniles." The average American adult believes that youths commit 43 percent of all violent crime in the U.S., three times the true figure of 13 percent—and, as a result, a large majority is eager to harshly punish juveniles.

Responsible journalists would be looking to reverse this dangerous misimpression they have helped create. Just the opposite is occurring.

In the scare campaign against adolescents, the news media not only uncritically repeat official claims, they actively embellish them with sinister cover stories and apocalyptic tales of suburban mayhem. The message is screamed from headlines, magazine covers, and network specials: Adolescents are "wild in the streets" (*Newsweek*, 8/2/92); teens everywhere are "killer kids" (*Reader's Digest*, 6/93).

Though casting a few paeans to details like poverty, discrimination and abuse, the media scare campaign declares that violence is innate to teenagers and coming mayhem is inevitable. Therefore, the only real solution, articulated by former Robert Kennedy aide Adam Walinsky (*Atlantic*, 7/95), is spending tens of billions to hire five million more police officers and suspending basic civil rights to combat the "epidemic of teen violence."

Unnatural Aggression

The problem with the 1990s teen-violence scare campaign is not that its prediction of a more violent future is wrong—it may well be correct. The problem is its wrongheaded explanation for why violence is rising.

There is no such thing as "youth violence," any more than there is "black violence" or "Italian violence." The recent rise in violent crime arrests among youths is so clearly founded in social conditions, not age-group demographics, that experts and officials have had to strain mightily to ignore or downplay them.

The social scientists receiving the most media attention "argue that teenage aggression is natural" (*Newsweek*, 8/2/92). If it is, we would expect teens all over the world to be violent. That is far from the case.

Murder, the most reliably reported crime around the world, is typically committed by killers very close in age to their victims (unless the victims are children or the elderly). In the 19 largest industrial nations outside the U.S., the 40 million young males aged 15 to 24 committed just 800 murders in recent reporting years (World Health Organization, *World Health Statistics Annual*, 1994). In these other Western nations, which have a total of 7,100 murders a year, the typical killer is age 30 or older, far beyond the teen years.

In stark contrast, the U.S.'s 18 million 15-to-24-year-old males accounted for 6,800 murders in 1992. American murder peaks at age 19. U.S. 15-to-24-year-olds are 16 times more likely to be murdered than their counterparts in other Western nations. (U.S. adults have a seven times' greater murder risk.)

U.S. experts, politicians, and their media parroters couldn't be more wrong: There is nothing innately violent about teenagers. There is something extremely violent—hysterically so— about the United States. Not even similar "frontier cultures" such as Canada and Australia have murder tolls remotely approaching ours.

Clearly, there are reasons other than "teen age" that explain why nine out of 10 young men murdered in the world's 20 largest Western countries are Americans. Here American social scientists and the media dispense some of the most absurd escapisms as "explanations."

Favorite Villains

The favorite conservative and pop-psychology villain (from right-wing media critics like Michael Medved and William Bennett to officials of the Clinton administration) is media violence, and the cure-all is more restrictions on TV, movies, books and music available to youths. But the media in most other Western nations are as violent as America's or more so. Efforts by U.S. experts to explain why Japan has extraordinarily violent media but extraordinarily low societal violence (9 million Japanese teens accounted for just 35 murders in 1992) are the essence of lame. (See James Q. Wilson's illogic in the *Los Angeles Times*, 6/25/95.)

The favorite liberal scapegoat is America's gun proliferation. "Whereas illegal firearms were not easily available to 12 year-olds just a few years back, guns can now be obtained in any neighborhood by almost any youngster who has a yen for one," the *L.A. Times* reported (9/9/95), summing up expert opinion. The panacea is another age-based restriction: tougher laws to keep guns away from youths.

True, Europeans and Japanese do not routinely pack heat. And Californians, in a state with 4,000 murders in 1994, purchase 300,000 to 400,000 handguns every year.

But if violent media and guns "in every neighborhood" were the reasons for teen violence, we would expect affluent white families to have the most murderous kids. White households are nearly twice as likely to harbor guns, and one-third more likely to subscribe to blood-dripping cable TV channels, than black and other nonwhite households (*Statistical Abstract of the U.S. 1995*). Yet in California, where whites are the plurality race, nonwhites account for 87 percent of all teen homicides and 80 percent of all teen arrests for violent crimes.

How do those who blame media violence, gun availability, and/or "inherent teenage aggression" explain that?

Poverty Violence

The major factor, buried in teen-violence stories and rarely generating any remedies, is poverty. The biggest differences between the U.S. and the 19 other relatively peaceful industrial nations cited above are youth poverty and extreme disparities in income between rich and poor. The 1995 Luxembourg Income Study found the U.S. raises three to eight times more children in poverty than other Western nations. The U.S. has the largest and fastest-growing gap in income between its richest 5 percent and poorest 5 percent of any industrial society (*U.S. News*, 8/28/95).

One figure summarizes the real U.S. violence issue. In 1993, 40 million Americans lived below the official poverty line (which itself understates the true rate of poverty). Half of these are children, and six in ten are non-white. While most impoverished people are not violent, there is no question among criminologists that the stresses of poverty are associated with much higher violent crime levels among all races and ages.

(That poverty is linked to crime should not come as a great surprise. After all, during the Great Depression murder spiraled upward—peaking in 1933 with a rate of 9.7 murders per 100,000, higher than 1993's 9.5 per 100,000 rate. See U.S. Census Bureau, *Historical Statistics of the United States*.)

If you divide the number of violent crimes by the number of people living in destitution, the phenomenon of "teenage violence" disappears: Adjusted for poverty, 13-to-19-year-olds have almost the same crime rate as people in their 40s, and have a crime rate well below that of those in their 20s and 30s. (Bureau of Justice Statistics, *Sourcebook of Criminal Justice Statistics 1994*; U.S. Census Bureau, *Poverty in the United States*, 1993).

The same adjustment for poverty sheds light on an issue that moderates and liberals seem afraid to discuss—the disproportionate amount of crime committed by non-white teens. "It's increasingly clear that everyone's kids are at risk," the Rand Corporation's Peter Greenwood told the *L.A. Times* (9/6/95)—which reprinted the meaningless comment under the blaring headline, "A New Wave of Mayhem."

Neither Greenwood nor the *Times* explained why, if "everyone's kids are at risk," a black youth is 12 times more likely to be murdered than a white youth, or why 31 California counties with a combined population of 2.5 million reported zero teen murders in 1993 (California Center for Health Statistics, 1995).

In fact, teen murder rates for whites are low and falling; non-white teen murder rates are high and rising. In 1975, 97 white youths and 240 nonwhite (including Hispanic) youths were arrested for homicide in California. In 1994, homicide arrests among white youths had fallen to 60, but among non-white youths had doubled to 482 (*Crime & Delinquency in California*, 1975-1993, and 1994 printout).

But notwithstanding Charles Murray's racist *Bell Curve* theories, non-white "dysgenics" is not the explanation for the disparity. If one adjusts the racial crime rate for the number of individuals living in extreme poverty, non-whites have a crime rate similar to that of whites at every age level.

The raging anecdotal campaign to portray affluent youths as out of control (see *New York Times* Magazine, 10/8/95; *Los Angeles Times*, 9/6/95), and the far-out-of-proportion hype accorded the pathetic suburban Lakewood Spur Posse, are attempts to hide the fact that the issue is the same as it always has been: poverty and racism.

Masking the Issues

Why is "teen violence" deployed by politicians and experts through a compliant media to mask the real issue of "poverty violence?" Because in Washington, as *U.S. News & World Report* notes (11/6/95), "reducing child poverty, much less eradicating it, is no longer a paramount priority for either political party."

Instead, the focus is on the sort of proposals put forward by the conservative Council on Crime in America (*Reuters*, 1/16/96): more police, more prisons, longer sentences imposed at younger ages. That states like California, Texas and Oklahoma have imposed exactly such get-tough measures for two decades and suffered record increases in violent crime appears to have little impact on the debate.

We don't want to spend the money to reduce youth poverty. But blaming concocted "innate" teenage traits for violence opens up a wide array of political and agency profiteering to "treat" the problem. Admitting that the issue might be that 45 percent of black youth, and 40 percent of Hispanic youth, grow up in poverty is not on the official agenda—so it is not on the news media's, either.

CHAPTER 3

Media and
Youth Violence

Chapter Preface

The rise of new technologies during the twentieth century changed the face of the American media forever. News that used to take weeks to travel across the country became instantly accessible with the introduction of radio, television, and the Internet. Over the years, violent images became a part of our daily lives as movies and television shows continually pushed the boundaries of what society considered acceptable. Some critics argue that such images can be confusing, especially to young children, while others feel that violent images in the media are harmless because most people can tell the difference between fantasy and reality.

The debate over violence in the media and its affect on young people can be traced back to the 1950s when parents and educators became concerned over the "inappropriate material" found in comic books. A Senate Subcommittee was formed to examine the problem. Testimony from researchers and psychologists even led to the formation of the Comics Code Authority, which tried to regulate the content of comic books.

This would not be the last time that the government heard testimony concerning violence in the media. In the 1970s, a Senate Subcommittee published a report stating that violence in the movies and on television was a major factor in many crimes.

In the 1980s, the focus of concern shifted from movies and television to music. Many parents and political officials felt that rap and rock music contained unnecessarily violent lyrics as well as references to drugs and sex. In an effort to regulate the sale of such music to children and teens, a group of mothers in Washington, D.C. formed the Parents Music Resource Center (PMRC). Many of these women were the wives of politicians and they brought their fight for tougher regulations to the Senate floor. Although the government backed away from censorship, the PMRC has had a lasting effect on the music industry. Parental advisory stickers warn parents that certain CDs contain material that might be inappropriate for children.

Other efforts to involve the government in enforcing stricter regulations concerning violence in the media have been less successful. In the 1990s several studies suggested that violent television shows, movies, and video games were key contributors to violence among American children and teenagers. These studies were reviewed by the Senate Committee on the Judiciary, which stated that though violence in the media was increasing, it was the job of parents, not the government, to monitor the type of media their children were exposed to.

Of course, not everyone favored the censorship of violence in the media. Many people felt that violence in the media was merely a form of creative expression. As video games became more graphic and realistic during the 1990s, some people worried that these games were blurring the lines between fantasy and reality for young and impressionable adolescents. Avid video game players argue that the games they play are actually a healthy way to release any aggressive feelings they feel.

As the Internet became an integral part of children's lives at the beginning of the new millennium, parents were legitimately concerned about the websites their kids visited. Though violent images were available online, children faced another alarming threat when they logged onto the World Wide Web. School bullies were now using the Internet to terrorize their victims online. The problem became so rampant in some schools that many established anti-bullying policies that also cover Internet harassment.

The debate over the influence that the media has on youth violence still exists today and will most likely continue to be an issue of major concern for years to come.

The "Crime" of Comic Books

Fredric Wertham

Before the Internet and cable television, another form of media was shouldering the blame for the increasing number of youths involved in crime and violence. In the 1950s, many parents and authority figures became increasingly concerned about the violent images depicted in the pages of comic books. They feared that children that read comics were becoming desensitized to real life violence and would not be able to understand the difference between fantasy and reality. A Senate Subcommittee on Juvenile Delinquency was organized, bringing in experts from several fields of study to testify on the problem of youth violence. Dr. Fredric Wertham, a psychiatrist interested in the effects of mass media on children, argued that comic books truly did have a negative impact on the impressionable minds of America's youth. During his testimony, Wertham presented the findings of a study concerning the correlation between comic books and youth violence. The doctor argued that comic books could be a major contributing factor to the continued increase in violence and aggression in young people. However, instead of censorship, Wertham felt that parental supervision was the best form of prevention. Wertham's most famous work was a book on the influence of comic books on America's youth entitled Seduction of the Innocent.*

O n April 21, 1954, Dr. [Fredric] Wertham presented his testimony before the Senate Subcommittee on Juvenile Delinquency, from which the following extracts are taken.

"My opinion is based on clinical investigations which I started in the winter of 1945 and 1946. They were carried out not by me alone, but with the help of a group of associates,

Fredric Wertham, "Do the Crime Comic Books Promote Juvenile Delinquency?" Testimony before the Senate Subcommittee on Juvenile Delinuency, April 21, 1954.

psychiatrists, child psychiatrists, psycho-analysts, social workers, psychiatric social workers, remedial reading teachers, probation officers, and others.

"In addition to material seen at the clinic both at Queens and Lafargue, we have studied whole school classes, whole classes of remedial reading clinics, over 300 children in a parochial school and private patients and consultations.

"To the best of my knowledge our study is the first and only individual large-scale study on the subject of comic books in general.

"The methods that we have used are the ordinary methods used in psychiatry, clinical interviews, group interviews, intelligence tests, reading tests, projective tests, drawings, the study of dreams, and so on.

"This research was a sober, painstaking, laborious clinical study, . . . since it has been going on now for 7 years.

"In addition to that we have read all that we could get hold of that was written in defense of comics, which is almost a more trying task than reading the comic books themselves.

"What is in comic books? In the first place, we have completely restricted ourselves to comic books themselves. That leaves out newspaper comic strips entirely.

"I must say, however, that when some very harmless comic strips for children printed in newspapers are reprinted for children in comic books, you suddenly can find whole pages of gun advertisements which the newspaper editor would not permit to have inserted in the newspaper itself.

"There have been, we have found, arbitrary classifications of comic books according to the locale where something takes place.

"We have found that these classifications don't work if you want to understand what a child really thinks or does.

"We have come to the conclusion that crime comic books are comic books that depict crime and we have found that it makes no difference whether the locale is western or space ship.

"If a man is killed he is killed whether he comes from Mars or somewhere else, and we have found, therefore, two large groups, the crime comic books and the others.

"Now, nobody versed in any of this type of clinical research would claim that comic books alone are the cause of juvenile delinquency. It is my opinion, without any reasonable doubt, and without any reservation, that comic books are an important contributing factor in many cases of juvenile delinquency.

Crime Comics and Kids

"There arises the question: What kind of child is affected? I say again without any reasonable doubt and based on hundreds and hundreds of cases of all kinds, that it is primarily the normal child.

"American children are wonderful children. If we give them a chance they act right. It is senseless to say that all these people who get into some kind of trouble with the law must be abnormal or there must be something very wrong with them.

"As a matter of fact, the most morbid children that we have seen are the ones who are less affected by comic books because they are wrapped up in their own fantasies.

"Now, it is said also in connection with this question of who reads comic books and who is affected by them, it is said that children from secure homes are not affected.

"As long as the crime comic books industry exists in its present forms there are no secure homes. Must you not take into account the neighbor's children?

"Now, the effect of comic books operates along four lines. While in our studies we had no arbitrary age limit, I am mostly interested in the under 16 and the first effect that is very early manifested is an effect in general on the ways of living with people. That is to say, on theoretical development.

"One of the outstanding things there is in crime comic books—let me say here that in my opinion crime comic books, as I define them, are the overwhelming majority of all comic books at the present time, is an endless stream of brutality. I would take up all your time if I would tell you all the brutal things.

Comics Create Confusion

"I think that comic books primarily, and that is the greatest harm they do, cause a great deal of ethical confusion.

"I would like to give you a very brief example. There is a school in a town in New York State where there has been a great deal of stealing. Some time ago some boys attacked another boy and they twisted his arm so viciously that it broke in two places, and, just like in a comic book, the bone came through the skin.

"In the same school about 10 days later 7 boys pounced on another boy and pushed his head against the concrete so that the boy was unconscious and had to be taken to the hospital. He had a concussion of the brain.

"Now this is what I call ethical and moral confusion. Here is a general moral confusion. Not all of them, but most of them, are very great comic book readers, have been and are.

"Many of these things happen and it is my belief that the comic book industry has a great deal to do with it. While I don't say it is the only factor at all, it may not be the most important one, it is one contributing factor.

"The second avenue along which comic books contribute to delinquency is by teaching the technique and by the advertisements for weapons. If it were my task to teach children delinquency, to tell them how to hurt people, how to break into stores, how to cheat, how to forge, how to do any known crime, if it were my task to teach that, I would have to enlist the crime comic book industry. I will say that every crime of delinquency is described in detail and that if you teach somebody the technique of something you, of course, seduce him into it.

"I know of no more erroneous theory about child behavior than to assume that children must be predisposed to do anything wrong. I think there is a hairline which separates a boy who dreams about that, dreams about such a thing, and the boy who does it.

"Now, I don't say, and I have never said, and I don't believe it, that the comic-book factor alone makes a child do anything.

"You see, the comic-book factor only works because there are many, many other factors in our environment, not necessarily the homelife, not necessarily the much-blamed mother, but there are many other things; the other boys in school, the newspaper headlines where everybody accuses the other one of being a liar or thief. There are many, many other factors in our lives. In most cases this factor works with other factors, but there are many cases that I know where such crimes have been committed purely as imitation and would have never been committed if the child hadn't known this technique.

"In other words, I want to stress for you what we have found, that the temptation, and, of course, we know it from our ordinary lives—that temptation and seduction is an enormous factor. We don't have to be materially bad to do something bad occasionally, and, moreover, these children who commit such a delinquency, they don't do that because they are bad. They don't even necessarily do it to get the money or to get even, but it is a glorious deed.

"You go there, you show how big you are. You are almost as big as these people you read about in crime comic books.

"The third avenue where they do harm is by discouraging children. Many of these comic books, crime-comic books, and many of the other ones have ads which discourage children and give them all kinds of inferiority feelings. They sell them all kinds of medicines and gadgets. The children spend a lot of money and they get very discouraged, they think they are too big, too little, or too heavy. They think this bump is too big, or too little.

"These discouraged children are very apt to commit delinquency as we know and have known for a long time.

"Now, the fourth avenue I shall not go into in detail because that includes not only the crime-comic books, but that includes all comic books.

Comics Contribute to Other Problems

"We have found all comic books have a very bad effect on teaching the youngest children the proper reading technique, to learn to read from left to right. This balloon print pattern prevents that. So many children, we say they read comic books, they don't read comic books at all. They look at pictures and every once in a while, as one boy expressed it to me, 'When they get the woman or kill the man then I try to read a few words,' but in any of these stories you don't have to have any words. In other words, the reading is very much interfered with.

"Now, it is a known fact, although it is not sufficiently emphasized, that many delinquents have reading disorders, they can't read well. There have been estimates as to how many delinquents have reading disorders.

"We have found over and over again that children who can't read are very discouraged and more apt to commit a delinquency.

"We have isolated comic books as one factor. A doctor tries to isolate one factor and see what it does and tries to correlate it with other factors which either counteract it or help it or run parallel.

"In my opinion this is a public-health problem. I think it ought to be possible to determine once and for all what is in these comic books and I think it ought to be possible to keep the children under 15 from seeing them displayed to them and preventing these being sold directly to children.

"Now, in conclusion, I detest censorship. I believe that what is necessary for children is supervision."

Violence in Media Encourages Real Violence

Senate Committee on the Judiciary

As youth violence increased in the 1990s, the government started searching for some sort of explanation for the growing problem. Data from several research studies and polls were collected and analyzed by the Senate Committee on the Judiciary. The report, released in 1999, outlines what this committee believes to be the key factors that contribute to youth violence in the United States. With statistical evidence as support, the senate committee argues that all forms of media—television, movies, music, video games, and the Internet—significantly contribute to the epidemic of youth violence in America. They assert that an increase in the number of violent images and lyrics that children are exposed to has a direct correlation to the increase of violence and aggression in the country's young people. After outlining and explaining the Juvenile Justice Act, the committee points out that though media is regulated by the government, the primary reason youth violence continues is that parents do not monitor the media that their children are exposed to.

American media are exceedingly violent. With television, analysis of programming for 20 years (1973 to 1993) found that over the years, the level of violence in prime-time programming remained at about 5 violent acts per hour. An August 1994 report by the Center for Media and Public Affairs reported that in one 18-hour day in 1992, observing 10 channels of all major kinds of programs, 1,846 different scenes of violence were noted, which translated to more than 10 violent scenes per hour, per channel, all day. A follow-up study conducted in 1994, found a 41 percent increase in violent scenes

Senate Committee on the Judiciary, "Children, Violence, and the Media: A Report for Parents and Policy Makers," September 14, 1999.

to 2,605, which translated to almost 15 scenes of violence per hour. Like television, our cinemas are full of movies that glamorize bloodshed and violence, and one need only listen to popular music radio and stroll down the aisle of almost any computer store to see that our music and video games are similarly afflicted.

Not only are our media exceedingly violent; they are also ubiquitous. The percentage of households with more than one television set has reached an all-time high of 87 percent, and roughly 1/2 of American children have a television set in their room. Forty-six percent of all homes with children have access to at least one television set, a VCR, home video game equipment and a personal computer, and 88.7 percent of such homes have either home video game equipment, a personal computer, or both.

What does that mean for our children? Most children now have unprecedented technological avenues for accessing the "entertainment" our media industries provide. The average 7th grader watches about 4 hours of television per day, and 60 percent of those shows contain some violence. The average 7th grader plays electronic games at least 4 hours per week, and 50 percent of those games are violent. According to the American Psychiatric Association, by age 18 an American child will have seen 16,000 simulated murders and 200,000 acts of violence.

The Littleton, Colorado school massacre has spawned a national debate over how to respond to this culture of media violence. In May 1999, a USA Today/CNN/Gallup poll found that 73 percent of Americans believe that TV and movies are partly to blame for juvenile crime. A TIME/CNN poll found that 75 percent of teens 13 to 17 years of age believe the Internet is partly responsible for crimes like the Littleton shootings, 66 percent blame violence in movies, television, and music, and 56 percent blame video game violence.

A Solid Link Between Media Violence and Violent Actions

In response, many, including the President, have called for studies to determine what effect that culture has on our children. Yet, we should not use such studies to dodge our responsibility to the American people. At least with respect to television and movies, existing research already demonstrates a solid link between media violence and the violent actions of our youth. Dr. Leonard D. Eron, a senior research scientist and professor of psychology at the University of Michigan, has estimated that television alone is responsible for 10 percent of youth violence. "The debate is over," begins a position paper on media violence by the American Psychiatric Association, "[f]or the last three decades, the one predominant finding in research on the mass media is that exposure to media portrayals of violence increases aggressive behavior in children." In the words of Jeffrey McIntyre, legislative and federal affairs officer for the American Psychological Association, "To argue against it is like arguing against gravity. . . ."

Some experts also believe that children can become addicted to violence. "Violence is like the nicotine in cigarettes," states Lt. Col. Dave Grossman, a former Green Beret and West Point psychology professor who now heads the Killology Research Group. "The reason why the media has to pump ever more violence into us is because we've built up a tolerance. In order to get the same high, we need ever-higher levels. . . . The television industry has gained its market share through an addictive and toxic ingredient."

Not surprisingly, many have come to view television and film violence as a national public health problem. The American Academy of Pediatrics, for instance, recently published a report advocating a national media education program to mitigate the negative impact of the harmful media messages seen and heard by children and adolescents. Robert Lichter, president of the Center for Media and Public Affairs, a nonprofit research group in Washington, D.C., has framed the issue in language we can all understand: "If you're worried about what your kid eats, you should worry about what your kid's watching."

Violence Pervades All Media

Less research has been done on the effect of music, video games, and the Internet on children. Nonetheless, on the basis of both that research and the research findings concerning television and film, experts confidently predict that violent music, video games, and Internet material also will be found to have harmful effects on children. . . .

Inadequate attention has been paid to the effect on children of violent music lyrics. Although no studies have documented a cause-and-effect relationship between violent lyrics and aggressive behavior, studies do indicate that a preference for heavy metal music may be a significant marker for alienation, substance abuse, psychiatric disorders, suicide risk, sex-role stereotyping, or risk-taking behaviors during adolescence. In addition, a Swedish study has found that adolescents who developed an early interest in rock music were more likely to be influenced by their peers and less influenced by their parents than older adolescents. . . .

We must not ignore the fact that these violent, misogynist images may ultimately affect the behavior and attitudes of many young men toward women. Writing about such lyrics in 1996, William J. Bennett, Senator Joseph Lieberman, and C. DeLores Tucker posed the following question: "What would you do if you discovered that someone was encouraging your sons to kill people indiscriminately, to find fun in beating and raping girls, and to use the word 'motherf—er' at least once in every sentence?" While the authors directed that question specifically to parents, it is best addressed to all Americans.

Violent Media Is Now Interactive

Interactive video games and the Internet have become the entertainment of choice for America's adolescents. Nearly seven in ten homes with children now have a personal computer (68.2 percent), and 41 percent of homes with children have access to the Internet. Annual video game revenues in the United States exceed $10 billion, nearly double the amount of money Americans spend going to the movies. On average, American children who have home video game machines play with them about 90 minutes a day.

The video games of choice for our youth are those that contain depictions of violence. A 1993 study, for instance, asked 357 seventh- and eighth-graders to select their preferences among five categories of video games. Thirty-two percent of the children selected the category "fantasy violence," and 17 percent selected "human violence." Only 2 percent of the children chose "educational games."

Parents are concerned that the fantasy violence in video games could lead their children to real-world violence. That concern intensified when Americans learned that the two juveniles responsible for the Littleton massacre had obsessively played the ultra-violent video game "Doom." Americans also recalled that the 14-year-old boy who shot eight classmates in Paducah, Kentucky in 1997, had been an avid player of video games. As the New York Times observed, "the search for the cause in the Littleton shootings continues, and much of it has come to focus on violent video games."

Here, too, the concern of parents is justified. Studies indicate that violent video games have an effect on children similar to that of violent television and film. That is, prolonged exposure of children to violent video games increases the likelihood of aggression. Some authorities go even further, concluding that the violent actions performed in playing video games are even more conducive to aggressive behavior. According to this view, the more often children practice fantasy acts of violence, the more likely they are to carry out real-world violent acts. As Professor Brian Stonehill, creator of the media studies program at Pomona College in Claremont, California, states: "The technology is going from passive to active. The violence is no longer vicarious with interactive media. It's much more pernicious and worrisome." Another researcher characterizes such games as sophisticated simulators, similar to those used in military training.

Equally troubling, video games often present violence in a glamorized light. Typical games cast players in the role of a shooter, with points scored for each "kill." Furthermore, advertising for such games often touts the violent conduct as a selling point—the more graphic and extreme, the better. For example, the advertisement for the game "Destrega" reads: "Let the slaughter begin"; and for the game "Subspace," "Meet people from all over the world, then kill them." As the popularity and graphic nature of such games increase, so does the harm to our youth. As Lt. Col. Dave Grossman bluntly warns, "We're not just teaching kids to kill. We're teaching them to like it. . . ."

Violence for Sale

The story is maddeningly similar for video games, the Internet, and music. The National Institute on Media and Family found that, despite the rating system in place for video games, in 1998, only 21 percent of retail and rental stores had any policies prohibiting the sale or rental of adult games to minors. Earlier this year the Senate Commerce Committee heard testimony about a 12-year-old boy who bought the video games "Doom" and "Quake"—both of which are rated for adults only—at a Washington, D.C. video store at the recommendation of the store clerk. The National Institute on Media and the Family also found that some manufacturers of video games are marketing to children ultra-violent products rated only for adults. One such video game, "Resident Evil 2," was advertised in the magazine "Sports Illustrated for Kids. . . ."

Former United States Senator Paul Simon observed several years ago that "Thirty seconds of a soap bar commercial sells soap. Twenty-five minutes worth of glorification of violence sell violence." Hence, having fed our children death and horror as entertainment, we should not be surprised by the outcome. But we are not powerless to address the problem. Americans need to respond to the problem of media violence in a responsible manner. If we take steps at both the national level—by dealing with the marketing of, and access to, violent media—and at the most local of levels—by empowering parents to exercise greater control over the material their children access—we can significantly reduce the impact of violent media on our young people.

Prevention Instead of Punishment

With respect to national reform, the Senate recently adopted the "Violent and Repeat Juvenile Offender Accountability and Rehabilitation Act of 1999" (the "Juvenile Justice Act"). This legislation, summarized below, adopts a comprehensive approach which confronts youth violence on several fronts, including media violence.

The Juvenile Justice Act implements a comprehensive strategy aimed at addressing the problem of juvenile violence. The legislation devotes substantial resources to state and local governments for the continued development and implementation of innovative and effective accountability and prevention programs. . . .

The act begins to confront what experts consider a principal cause of juvenile violence: depictions of violence in the media. The relevant provisions, summarized below, seek to reduce children's exposure to media violence by encouraging corporate responsibility and empowering parents. . . .

While the Juvenile Justice Act represents a promising start, much more needs to be done to reduce media violence. Further steps should be animated by the two imperatives that underlie the Juvenile Justice Act: encouraging corporate responsibility and empowering parents. Many media executives appear sincere in expressing their concerns about media violence. Thus, absent signs that this optimistic view of the industry is mistaken, policy proposals should facilitate, rather than compel, the exercise of corporate responsibility. As for parents, it bears repeating that they remain our most promising allies in this effort. Public policy initiatives therefore must empower them to fulfill their protective responsibilities. . . .

It's Not Just What's Taken Away . . .

Parents should know that the impact on children of television, movies, music, video games, and the Internet arises not only from the kinds of behavior they promote, but also from the other activities they replace. A Canadian study analyzed the changes in how families living in a small town spent their days before and after television was introduced. The study found that after television became available, people spent less time talking, socializing outside the home, doing household tasks, engaging in leisure activities, and being involved in community activities. People even slept less once the television entered the home. The lesson: Parents should supply their children with alternatives to television, movies, music, video games, and the Internet. Regularly providing things such as art supplies, books to read, athletic activities, or outdoor excursions will reduce the number of arguments about what to watch on television and teach children how to enjoy a broader range of activities.

Rap Music Gets a Bad "Rap"

Ivette M. Yee

Once thought of as a musical fad that was sure to fade, rap music has become a major part of popular culture. The phenomenon's influence is not just limited to music—rap affects everything from movies to video games to fashion. In the following selection, Ivette M. Yee traces the short history of rap music from its beginnings in a DJ's apartment in the Bronx to the billion dollar industry it has become today. Yee briefly explores rap's most popular topics—misogyny and violence—which have been blamed for having negative influences on America's youth. Yee asserts that though rap has a much broader horizon of topics dealing with issues like political expression and social consciousness, songs that focus on tamer topics rarely get exposure on the radio or cable music channels. According to Yee, rap gets a bad "rap," when in reality the genre does much to spread awareness of the rarely represented politics of poor black Americans. Yee is a staff writer for the South Florida Sun-Sentinel.

Love it or dis' it, rap music is here to stay, and so is hip-hop, the cultural force that surrounds it.

After a quarter-century, the music and its image have become a monster phenomenon, one that crosses racial, ethnic and socio-economic boundaries, influencing the clothes people wear, the entertainment they seek and the language they speak.

Rap music is now popular music, and hip-hop is a $10 billion industry with its influence evident everywhere.

Hang outside a movie theater and chances are you'll see young people sporting Sean John shirts (from rapper P. Diddy's clothing line), [and] boasting their "bling bling," (shiny jewelry).

Now rap's reach touches academia, with universities offering classes about rap music and hip-hop culture.

Rap Classes

"It's a big part of campus culture, huge," said Reginald Jolly, music director of the online music channel at Florida Atlantic University. "A lot of clubs on campus have functions and fund-raisers that are for the hip-hop crowd. So many people here listen to it."

FAU's first Hip-Hop Symposium will be conducted Saturday, with visiting professors and students discussing how rap relates to politics, black liberation, violence and social change.

Yet despite its popularity, the musical genre that has empowered countless youth and enraged adults over the last 25 years, always seems to get a bad rap.

Rap was born in the South Bronx in the '70s as dance-party music with spoken lyrics improvised over a series of beats in the African storytelling tradition. Hip-hop—the break-dancing, graffiti and DJ'ing that became associated with rap—was born in the mid-1970s when DJ Kool Herc began throwing block parties in the Bronx and experimenting with the new music and twin turntables.

In the 1980s and early '90s, rap infused political messages and stressed social consciousness, delving into African Americans' struggle for equality.

Then came "gangsta rap," a sonic barrage, which emphasized guns, drugs and fearlessness in the ghetto.

"Rap has always been controversial, with a long history of violence that has obscured the more positive messages," said Richard Shusterman, a philosopher and FAU professor who has written essays about rap.

Not Just About Violence

These days, more of the music is about excess—in fortune, in sex and in hit records—but rap never has shaken its reputation as a misogynistic and violent form of music.

Some say the labels are unmerited.

"There's also been a long and honorable tradition of songs urging people to stop the violence," Shusterman said, "but those don't get the play time."

Both the media and record companies have been blamed for spotlighting only certain kinds of rap—"gangsta" rap or glamour-rap—and contributing to a limited view of the music, both rappers and scholars say.

For some, it's a circumstance as old as rap itself.

Art Imitates Life

"Being that it is an urban art form that came from the streets, it's always going to get looked at with a suspicious eye and have a stigma attached to it," said New York-based rapper, Cormega, a former Def Jam recording artist who now runs his own label and recently released his critically-praised album The Testament. "It is just one of those injustices that is always going to be there."

Sujatha Fernandes, a lecturer at Princeton University who focuses on rap and political expression in a global context and a speaker at Saturday's symposium, said studying rap and hip-hop opens a window into the younger generation that's been raised outside the social stability of the '50s and early '60s, in a world riddled with poverty and violence.

"People think that hip-hop perpetuates violence, but it really reflects many aspects of the culture," Fernandes said. "What I have a problem with is critics that see hip-hop as the sole deliverer of misogynistic messages, instead of looking at all of the other spheres where sexism does exist."

Rap Did Not Invent Evil

Rap is not the deliverer of all evils or the first to portray them, others said.

"Rap doesn't have the monopoly on the aesthetic presentation of violence. Movies and TV are filled with it and there's always been an artistic representation of it, from early plays like Oedipus and King Lear to the depiction of Christ's crucifixion, which are all over art," Shusterman said.

For universities such as FAU, recognizing the importance of rap and hip-hop gives the music and the culture added credibility.

"I think it shows that rap is finally getting the respect and attention it deserves," Cormega said.

It also creates exposure for those artists who rhyme to their own beat, rapping for a greater cause despite the lack of radio play and media attention.

"There are all different kinds of rap artists out there. We're living proof," said Posdnuos of De La Soul, the eclectic and alternative hip-hop trio which made a name for itself in the late '80s and still is touring.

"There's also rappers like Common, Mos Def and Goodie Mob that have something important to say.

"If you study rap, you learn the history of it and how it enriches people's lives. Just through the words, rappers are going through therapy, talking about their lives and their experiences," Posdnuos said.

Widespread Censorship of Violence is Necessary

Dave Grossman and Gloria DeGaetano

In the 1990s studies showed a marked increase in the number of violent shows marketed towards children. From cartoons to live-action adventures, violence was used in physical comedy situations and as a tool to make shows seem more exciting to children. Researchers pointed to a relationship between the number of violent images children are exposed to and an increase in aggression. They also pointed out that feelings of terror increased among youths. In the following article, Dave Grossman argues that violence on TV breeds violence in the minds of our nation's children. Grossman highlights evidence he feels illustrates the problems of allowing children to watch these shows. He explains the ill effects these programs have on both the children that watch them and the adults that try to shelter their kids from an increasingly volatile world. He argues that more censorship is needed on the small screen to help protect the mental well-being of the country's young people. Grossman is a professor of psychology and military science at West Point.

Scientific evidence over whelmingly supports media violence as a major, significant factor contributing to real-life violence in our society—and we'll prove it. It's a lot to absorb—the findings of key studies in the last fifty years—but it is of paramount importance that people understand just how much hard evidence exists on the subject. . . .

We should be clear from the outset: the studies implicate media violence as a major influence; none indict it as the only cause of real-life aggression. Rather, what the studies demon-

Dave Grossman and Gloria DeGaetano, "Not Just a 'Toaster with Pictures,'" in *Stop Teaching Our Kids to Kill: A Call to Action against TV, Movie, and Video Game Violence*, New York: Crown Publishers, 1999. Copyright © by Dave Grossman and Gloria DeGaetano. Used by permission of Crown Publishers, a division of Random House, Inc.

strate is that violent imagery as a form of amusement for children and youth—who haven't fully developed their thinking functions, who need guidance to analyze and evaluate their experiences, and who have yet to develop accuracy in interpreting and describing feelings spurred by violent imagery—is at very least a dangerous proposition. If adults, with their thinking functions developed, with their abilities to analyze and evaluate intact, and with their language skills proficient enough to express the feelings brought up by horrific images, can still be quite disturbed by violence on-screen, imagine how children and teens are affected and infected. Ours is a media culture careening out of control, with violence everywhere we turn. Understanding the links between real life and screen violence is paramount to taking effective, long-lasting action.

In the myriad studies done over the last four decades, experts have found three basic negative effects from exposure to screen violence: increased aggression, fear, and insensitivity to real-life and screen violence. Some studies highlight one or more of these effects, and other more inclusive, long-term experiments touch on all three. . . .

An Increase in Aggression

The studies repeatedly demonstrate that we see more physical violence by children and youth who watch screen violence and/or play violent video games. It's that simple. As the content of television becomes more violent, so do our children. Since 1982, television violence has increased 780 percent and in that same time period teachers have reported a nearly 800 per cent increase of aggressive acts on the playground. Continual exposure, of course, has more long-lasting effects than short-term episodes. . . .

Even though social scientists had been studying the relationship between television and aggression for several decades, what is perhaps the most telling indictment did not come from social scientists, and it did not start as a study of television. By 1981, the rate of real-life violence had risen to the level where it was *finally* being identified as a public health issue. Dr. Brandon Centerwall, M.D., an epidemiologist, was asked to help start the violence research program at the National Centers for Disease Control in Atlanta, Georgia. A central issue confronting the research team was the doubling of the murder rate in the United States since the 1950s. That the rate had doubled was indisputable. The question was, why?

Dr. Centerwall approached this as a question of epidemiology, searching through rigorous statistical analysis for the causes of the "epidemic of violence." He considered every possibility that any research evidence had ever suggested might reasonably be a cause, including changes in urbanization and economic conditions; the effect of the post-World War II baby boom; trends in alcohol abuse, capital punishment, and civil unrest; changes in the availability of firearms; and television. Television was included as part of the array. It was not considered more likely to provide an explanation than any of the other proposed candidates.

Over seven years of research, first at the Centers for Disease Control and later at the University of Washington, Dr. Centerwall gathered statistical data and tested the various factors to see if a causal relationship with the rising level of violence could be identified. One by one, as the research evolved, factors were eliminated for significant causal relationships. Yet each time the television hypothesis was subjected to the testing, it quite stubbornly refused to be eliminated. As each of the other candidates dropped away, television slowly moved to front and center.

After testing rigorously for confounding cross-relationships with other possible causes, the conclusion was inescapable. And the process of arriving at the epidemiological conclusion was so gradual that, in Dr. Centerwall's words, "There never was a moment of 'Aha!' It simply happened."

After painstaking testing all over the world, Dr. Centerwall blew the roof off the subject by stating that if "television technology had never been developed, there would today be 10,000 fewer murders each year in the United States, 70,000 fewer rapes, and 700,000 fewer injurious assaults. . ."

Violence Desensitizes Us to Violence

Another effect of screen violence on children—and, for that matter, adults—is that they become more desensitized to violence and less outraged by its effects. Callousness toward brutality sets in and a "so what?" attitude begins to frame the context by which horrific acts are seen. Consequently, more justification for violence takes place in the minds of these individuals. Images of violence as "cool" serve to reinforce deviant attitudes and result in less empathy, compassion, and understanding for human suffering. . . .

Cultural insensitivity is also demonstrated by our increased ability to tolerate more and more graphic displays of violence in the media. Hyperviolent movies such as *Natural Born Killers*, *Pulp Fiction*, or *The Matrix* would not have been tolerated, let alone achieved commercial success, in 1939—the year that *Wuthering Heights*, *The Wizard of Oz*, and *Gone With the Wind* were released. PG-rated *Dick Tracy*, one of the more benign movies of the 1990s, with only fourteen slayings, had a higher body count than the original 1974 *Death Wish*, which by many people's standards was a really violent film. The definition of what is socially acceptable, even normal, alters according to our level of desensitization. "Simple" violence becomes passé; seeing a few dead bodies makes little or no impression on us. Body counts rise, violence is more graphic, real. And we soon start feeling comfortable with the kind of ultraviolence now seen regularly on television and at the movies. Another way we become desensitized to such violence is when it's presented without some kind of redeeming message. In 1990, social critic Mark Crispin Miller said this: "In *Bullitt* (1968) and *The*

French Connection (1971), in *The Searchers* (1956), and in movies of Sam Peckinpah, the violence, however graphic, was muted by a deep ambivalence that shadowed even the most righteous-seeming acts of vengeance, and that therefore suppressed the viewer's urge to join in kicking. In contrast, screen violence now is used primarily to invite the viewer to enjoy the feel of killing, beating, mutilating." The point being, viewing violence for its own sake is a destructive trend. Our children get nothing out of it except the message that violence is okay, even fun. . . .

Protecting Children from Terror

The third symptom of violence as entertainment is increased fear in our society. A constant diet of violent portrayals can make people more distrusting and exaggerate the threats of violence that really do exist. Nightmares and long episodes of anxious behavior are common for young children exposed to violence on TV or in a film.

Violent and/or scary TV programs and movies have both immediate and long-term effects on children. Immediate reactions include intense fear, crying, clinging behaviors, and stomachaches. Long-term reactions vary from nightmares and difficulty sleeping, concern about being hurt or killed, and aversion to common animals. . . .

Most of us protect our children from the violence that exists on the street, mainly because we don't want them to be physical victims of it but also because we are painfully aware of how exposure to it will skew their world perception. So what sense does it make for us to allow them to be saturated with images that frighten and terrorize? . . .

As our children were becoming more aggressive, desensitized, and fearful, TV violence continued to escalate. A 1994 study by the Center for Media and Public Affairs identified 1,846 violent scenes on network and cable programs between 6 A.M. and midnight on one day in Washington, D.C. Most of these were of an extremely horrific nature, and without context or judgment about social acceptability. The most violent periods were between 6 and 9 A.M., with 497 violent scenes, or 165.7 per hour, and between 2 and 5 P.M., with 609 violent scenes, or 203 per hour. These are the times of day when children and youth are most likely to be watching. This is no coincidence. The study also concluded that from 1992 to 1994 depictions of serious violence increased 67 percent, violence in promos and trailers almost doubled, and violence in network and local news programs increased 244 percent. . . .

Responses to the Evidence

[In] 1990, the Senate and the House passed the Children's Television Act, but President Bush refused to sign it, saying it bordered on infringement of the First Amendment. He did, however, allow it to become law. The Children's Television Act made two provisions:

1. Commercials during children's programs could not exceed 10.5 minutes per hour on weekends and 12 minutes per hour on weekdays.

2. Television broadcast licenses could not be renewed unless the station had complied with the first provision and had served the "educational and information needs of children" by providing at least three hours a week of educational programming. . . .

By 1992, the industry, . . . had established a set of guidelines. Within this venue, at this time, before this audience, they simply could not deny the many negative effects of TV violence any longer, and thus found themselves to be morally and legally obligated to construct what they called a "Statement of Principles." Note that, while Congress had demanded the establishment of a set of "guidelines," what the industry created were "principles." Being forced to establish guidelines (or principles) by no means forces the industry to follow them. Consider some of the following text and compare it to what you see on your television today. If you see a wide disparity, you're not alone.

- Children's programs should attempt to contribute to the sound, balanced development of children and to help them achieve a sense of the world at large;

- Violence, physical or psychological, should be portrayed only in a responsible manner and should not be used exploitatively. Where consistent with the creative intent, programs involving violence should present the consequences of violence to its victims and perpetrators;

- Presentation of the details of violence should avoid the excessive, the gratuitous, and the instructional;

- The use of violence for its own sake and the detailed dwelling upon brutality or physical agony, by sight or by sound, should be avoided;

- Particular care should be exercised where children are involved in the depiction of violent behavior.

The fact that the television industry came up with such principles strongly suggests they knew what they should be doing—what was right. But it doesn't take much research at this point to figure out that they ignored their own advice. And sure enough, more pressure from Congress and the threat of restrictive legislation prompted the cable industry to sponsor the three-year (1996–1998) National Television Violence Study (NTVS) at a cost of $3.5 million. (The broadcast industry, not to be outdone, also financed its own three-year study during this time period at a cost of $1.3 million.)

The National Cable Television Association (NCTA) awarded a three-year contract to Mediascope, Inc., to administer the largest study of television content ever undertaken. Mediascope, in association with the Universities of California, North Carolina, and Texas, was selected to conduct the research after a competitive process that attracted proposals from many leading experts in media research. . . .

The conclusion of the first year of the study was that "psychologically harmful" violence is pervasive on broadcast and cable TV programs. The NTVS found not only that 57 percent of programs contained some violence, but also that the context in which this violence occurs can have harmful effects.

In 1997, the second-year summary of the research was released, with similar results. And in April 1998, third-year results told the same story and made a mockery of the networks' "principles" and the so-called cooperation on the topic of reducing TV violence. . . .

Writing about the fallout from the industry-supported research. Dr. George Comstock, Newhouse Professor at the S. I. Newhouse School of Public Communication at Syracuse University, pointed out: "What had begun as a concern over the harmfulness of violent portrayals, and especially in regard to the facilitation of antisocial behavior on the part of viewers, became an endeavor simply to inform parents so that they could better govern their children's viewing. . . . The social and behavioral sciences have empirically identified a problem and offered a solution (however difficult): the reduction of harmful portrayals. If the problem is those . . . harmful effects, then labeling content for the V-chip exorcism will succeed only if all households comply. And if they were to do so, then there would be no need for the V-chip because the incentives to produce such content would be absent. The industry has substituted appearance for substance."

While U.S. network executives and film producers continued with wide-eyed innocence to plead ignorance of the vast amount of evidence, the rest of the world was penning their indictment for the perpetuation of the new "global aggressive culture" that was being marketed to children. . . .

Along with the science has come the advice from the experts in child development. Yet the industry has refused to listen both to the evidence and to the purveyors of that evidence. Pediatricians, psychologists, educators, and experts on youth violence have taken on the enormous responsibility of making the industry pay attention and make significant changes. The responsibility should be reversed. It is not up to the child-care experts to get the industry to listen. They have no leverage to do that. We need to realize that when it comes to our children's viewing habits, the *real* media critics are not Roger Ebert and other journalists but rather the AMA [American Medical Association], the APA [American Psychological Association], and the American Academy of Pediatrics. If the TV and movie industries truly had the interest of America's children in mind, they would actively engage the broad, mainstream consensus—not just hire a few "experts" who basically agree with them. The entertainment industry has taken the approach of "How much poison can we put in the food and get away with it?"

As a result of all this undeniable research, many experts and organizations with moral and social responsibility for children's welfare have issued strong statements over the years. When organizations representing all of America's doctors, all of her psychiatrists, and millions of parents, call upon an industry to change (i.e., reduce violence on the public airwaves), and then that industry does exactly the opposite (i.e., increases the violence), this can be viewed as nothing short of complete and total contempt for the people of the United States. . . .

Video Game Violence Is Harmless Fantasy

Ron Wilburn

As with television and movies, video games have become increasingly more violent over the years. Whereas gamers used to battle to rescue the princess from her evil captors, today's players purposely commit virtual acts of violent crime simply because they can. People are constantly placing the blame for violence and agression in teens on games like Grand Theft Auto, *which some argue actually trains children to kill. In the following selection, avid video-gamer Ron Wilburn attempts to set critics of video games straight in this letter to the editor. Wilburn, a sixteen-year-old student, researched the video game controversy for school and asserts that while video games do depict violence, they are still only games. The student points out that most teens are able to understand the difference between fantasy and reality, and that no video game will force a rational teen to kill. Wilburn suggests that video games are undeservedly blamed for inciting violence as well as other destructive behavior in young people. He argues that youth violence stems from a combination of complex situations and circumstances, and that no one factor is wholly responsible. Wilburn is from Belmont, Massachusetts. His letter first appeared in* Mothering *magazine.*

I am 16 years old and an avid video gamer. I have had many discussions with other gamers, as well as with adults, including my mom, who think that video games are bad for many reasons, including the idea that they encourage violence and promote obesity. I have loads of experience in the field of video games and have done research on the subject for school. I'd like to share my thoughts with you and perhaps encourage your readers to reconsider opinions they may hold on the effect video games have on families.

Undeserved Blame

All parents want their kids to be safe from violence and to behave in socially acceptable ways. Video games are sometimes blamed for violent behavior, from rough play in the school yard to the Columbine massacre. Some say that video games are training for murder, teaching adolescents that killing is easy and without consequence.

Sadly, in our society, violence is nothing new. Yet in the 20 years that video games have been around, the US crime rate, and specifically the rate of violent crime, has gone steadily down (Bureau of Statistics, www.ojp.usdoj.gov/bs/abstract/cnscj.htm), while video game use has soared. Also not new is the scapegoating of a single element to explain isolated events. Video games are a recent scapegoat, but others have been song lyrics, team sports, and various racial groups. Soon enough, video games will be forgotten as a source of violence and something else will be picked up.

The Absence of Video Games

In the wake of recent well-publicized violence in schools, the FBI compiled a list of potential indicators of violent behavior. These include: 1) a history of violent behavior, 2) alcohol or drug abuse, 3) lack of coping skills, 4) lack of a support system, 5) availability of a weapon. Other indicators are low self-esteem, cruelty to animals, lack of discipline, narcissistic personality, depression or flat affect, suicidal ideation, lack of remorse, easy manipulation by others, expressions of interest in previous shootings, a history of mental health treatment, and an interest in satanic or cult activities (www.knowgangs.com/school_resources/menu_019.htm). In such a comprehensive list, the absence of video games is significant. If the FBI thought video games were a threat, they would surely mention it.

In a 1999 report on mental health, the US surgeon general weighed in on youth violence and also failed to mention video games as a factor. Risk factors for violence that the report did mention were poverty, broken homes, and abusive or unsupportive parents (www.mentalhealth.org/youthviolence/surgeongeneral/SG_Site/chapter4/images/box_4-1.gif). This indicates that video games, a possible virtual outlet for violent feelings, are not responsible for the violence in today's youth. Family violence is the problem.

Moving Lights on a Dim Screen

While video games often portray violence, they are still only games: moving lights on a dim screen. Actual violence involves real people and real pain. Violent behavior is an outcome of a complex combination of social norms (www.hfg.org/hfg_review/4/adler-ga llant-2.htm) and is best understood and addressed by calm, thoughtful, open discussion rather than simplistic finger-pointing. Children raised in households that are fair and respectful become adolescents, and eventually adults, who are able to differentiate between reality and fantasy and between acceptable and unacceptable behavior, whether they play video games or not.

Ron Wilburn
Belmont, Massachusetts

Bullies in Cyberspace

Amanda Paulson

Bullying has long been a problem in schools across the country. For years, parents, students, and teachers have tried, and most often failed, to prevent students from tormenting other children in the classroom and the school yard. In the following selection, Amanda Paulson argues that many bullies have turned to the Internet while outside of school to continue the torture of their fellow classmates online. Paulson asserts that cyberbullying is a growing concern among teachers, parents, and school administrators. Paulson shows how bullies use the Internet to spread school rumors via email, instant-message embarrassing photos of unsuspecting teens, and post threats of violence against other students. Paulson points out that many of the bullies go unpunished, using the anonymity the World Wide Web provides to mask their true identities. The author examines this troubling new trend that often leaves teens feeling insecure and afraid to venture out into cyberspace. Paulson is the Midwest bureau chief of The Christian Science Monitor.

Hi-Tech Taunting

For one middle-school girl it was a rumor, circulated via text messaging, that she had contracted SARS [Severe Acute Respiratory Syndrome] while on a trip to Toronto. She returned to school and found nobody would come near her.

For an overweight boy in Japan, it was cellphone pictures, taken of him on the sly while he was changing in the locker room and then sent to many of his peers.

And for Calabasas High School in California, it was a website on which vicious gossip and racist and threatening remarks grew so rampant that most of the school was affected.

The actions themselves—rumors, threats, gossip, humiliation—are nothing new. But among today's adolescents—a generation of instant messengers, always connected, always wired—bullies are starting to move beyond slam books and whisper campaigns to e-mail, websites, chat rooms, and text messaging.

While in some ways it's no worse than old-fashioned bullying, cyberbullying has a few idiosyncrasies. Websites and screen names give bullies a mask of anonymity if they wish it, making them difficult to trace.

The pressure for kids to be always online means bullies can extend their harassment into their victims' homes.

And the miracle of the Web means that sharing an embarrassing photo or private note—with thousands of people—requires little more than the click of a key.

"It used to be if something happened at school, someone made a joke about you, or said something in front of you, that was horrible enough," says Glenn Stutzky, instructor in Michigan State University's School of Social Work.

"But at least a relatively small group of people is there and aware of it. With wireless technology, that stuff is much more quickly spread, not only around school but it has the potential of being put up and shared around the world."

No one knows that better than Ghyslain, the Canadian teenager who gained notoriety this year as "the Star Wars kid." Fooling around alone with a video camera one day, the somewhat awkward adolescent filmed himself acting out a scene from "Star Wars": He twirled and flung himself about the room, swinging a golf-ball retriever as his light saber. It was the sort of private geeky moment many kids have, but in Ghyslain's case, it went further.

Some peers got hold of the video, uploaded it to the Internet, and started passing it around. Doctored videos, splicing him into "The Matrix," "The Terminator," or the musical "Chicago," with added special effects and sounds, soon followed.

[He became] the most downloaded male of the year. According to news reports, he was forced to drop out of school and seek psychiatric help.

"It's one of the saddest examples," says Mr. Stutzky. "He did one goofy little thing, and now it will always be a part of that young man's life."

Cruel Messages—In an Instant

Most cyberbullying doesn't reach such extremes, but it's still damaging. One in 17 kids ages 10 to 17 had been threatened or harassed online, and about one-third of those found the incidents extremely distressing, according to a 2000 study by the University of New Hampshire's Crimes Against Children Research Center. A study in Britain by NCH, a British children's charity, found that 1 in 4 students had been bullied online.

The most common instances often involve instant messaging, or IM—the instantaneous chats that have spawned a lingo of their own and are a constant presence on most kids' computers. Bullies can send a mean or threatening IM with no identification beyond a selected screen-name. If that name gets blocked, they choose another.

More recently, it's cellphones. For several years now, bullying via text messaging and cellphone photos has been a concern in countries such as Britain and Japan, where such technologies are common. Stutzky says he's just beginning to see it in the US. He heard from a high-school boy who got text messages questioning his sexual orientation, and from a middle-school girl who got messages like: "Where did your mom get you those shoes? K-Mart?"

Other times, it's a website. Some circulate rumors, ask students to vote on the ugliest or fattest kid in school, or focus on one individual. When Will, a middle-schooler in Kansas, broke up with his girlfriend, she created a website devoted to smearing him.

She outlined vivid threats, made up vicious rumors, and described what it would be like to see him torn apart.

Photos are ammunition, too. Ted Feinberg, assistant director of the National Association of School Psychologists, often cites the young woman he met who had a falling out with a boy. In a fit of anger, he used photo-editing tools to paste her face onto a pornographic photo and sent it to his entire e-mail list.

"It was emotionally devastating for her" says Dr. Feinberg.

Bullies Hiding Behind Your Screen

The perpetrator was known, at least, in situations like the previous two. In Will's case, his mother went to the principal, the website came down, and the girl got counseling and was transferred to another school.

In other cases, however, schools feel helpless. Free-speech rights can make it difficult to take down a website, bullies are often anonymous, and most of the harassment takes place off school property. After the school shooting at Columbine High School in 1999, many schools began looking at bullying as a serious problem, and some instituted zero-bullying policies. But cyberspace is a new territory, and schools aren't sure how far to extend their jurisdiction.

J. Guidetti, principal of Calabasas High School, did get involved, after comments on [a website] caused many of his students to be depressed, angry, or simply unable to focus on school.

"It might have been happening off campus," says Mr. Guidetti, "but the effects carry on into the school day. . . . Our school had the most postings of any school in southern California. It became a snowball effect, like a real-life soap opera. It became this culture of its own, and got very hurtful very quickly."

The site has more than 30,000 members and any student can post a message. Guidetti first looked at [the website] after hearing about it from a parent. He was shocked to find some blatantly racist comments, threats, and even references to lynching certain students.

His next step was a series of meetings—with parents, students, and faculty—to keep everyone informed. But getting the site stopped, he learned, wasn't easy. Talking to law-enforcement officials led nowhere; there are few rules governing what can get posted on the Internet.

Eventually, a local radio station got involved and put enough pressure on the people running the site—a father-son duo—that they took it down in the spring [of 2003]. Already, there's [another website]—relatively harmless, so far. Guidetti checks it regularly for offensive content, one of the ever-growing tasks of a 21st-century principal.

Combating Cyberbullying

Despite the legal difficulties of forcing a website to shut down, or even discovering the identity of someone smearing or threatening another online, kids, parents, and schools do have ways to combat cyberbullying, experts say.

Perhaps the most important is simple communication. "You can buy filters and all these things, but I think the only filter that really works is between our kids' ears," says Bill Belsey, president of Bullying.org Inc., a nonprofit group in Canada. "We need to have really strong communication with our kids, so they know if they are ever being cyberbullied to come forward."

At www.cyberbullying.ca, a website that he runs, it details steps families can take—including how to track the owners of an e-mail address—and provides software that can help filter text or track e-mails.

He and others would like to see more corporate responsibility—Internet service providers taking down threatening sites, or at a minimum ISPs and cellphone companies providing clear policies against abuse and resources for reporting harassment. In Britain, notes Stutzky, cellphone companies already offer such resources and are developing software that sends copies of text messages to parents.

But some of the most effective techniques to fight cyberbullying are the same ones that fight bullying of any kind: Teach kids to report incidents. Don't engage the bully. Talk about the issues surrounding bullying at school and at home.

"It's not new bullying, it's just a vehicle," says Nancy Mullin-Rindler, director of the Project on Teasing and Bullying at Wellesley College in Massachusetts.

"The most effective responses are principals engaging parents and teachers to try to stop this sort of behavior," she adds. "There's this myth that we can't possibly know who does it. But you just have to use good old-fashioned sleuthing to find out. Kids want credit for doing this thing."

Online Bullying: A Punishable Offense

At Calabasas, Guidetti encourages the school's peer-support group to offer comfort and advice to victims of all sorts of bullying. John Gibbons, principal of Weston Middle School in Massachusetts, sent a listserv notice to parents [in December 2003], alerting them to instances of IM harassment among the students. He encouraged them to talk to their kids and gauge whether, in fact, they were mature enough to be using IM. . . .

"Some of them had no awareness of how much their kids were using it," he says. "For others, it prompted them to talk more about the content of the messages they send and receive."

More schools are sending home Internet use policies at the start of the school year and are including cyberbullying as an offense that can be punished.

Both parents and educators, notes Belsey, can help by showing kids the positive connections and educational benefits of the Internet.

"The promise of technology is absolutely brilliant," he says. "But we have to understand that the world our kids are growing up in is different than it was in the past. We can't condemn it, but need to give our kids enough information to cope with the world they're living in. . . . We need to show kids all the positive potential for teaching and learning that all this connectivity has."

CHAPTER 4

Responses to
Youth Violence

Chapter Preface

As it became apparent that youth violence was a problem that was not going to go away, members of society started searching for ways to deal with youthful offenders. The type of punishment that was suitable for young offenders became a rather sensitive issue for many in the justice system. Should children who act violently or commit murder be given special consideration because of their age?

Many people believed that child and teenage offenders should be treated differently. In the late 1800s, the juvenile justice system was established in the United States. The purpose of the system was to rehabilitate juvenile offenders so that they might someday be able to function as productive members of society. It was believed that young criminals would be more likely to benefit from rehabilitation than adults would. However, as youth violence continued throughout the 20th century, many questioned whether the system was really doing enough to help juvenile delinquents.

While the justice system dealt with the problem of youth violence in their own way, the medical community had another approach. In the early 1900s, researchers questioned whether youth violence was actually a mental disorder that could be treated. The Juvenile Psychopathic Institute was established in 1909 to examine young criminals and their mental health. Though the institute did not last long, the research completed there helped many researchers to better understand the minds of adolescents.

In the years to come, many people criticized the aging juvenile justice system for being unwilling to adapt with the times. Since its inception, the juvenile justice system treated all offenses committed by children, whether they were major or minor, in the same manner. It was not until the 1960s that the nature of the offender's crime was taken into account. In the

1980s, the seriousness of the crime also became a factor when considering what sort of punishment was necessary. Even today, the juvenile justice system continues to change and evolve in the way that it handles the nation's youngest criminals.

Even communities responded to the problem of youth violence in various ways. While some areas established neighborhood watch programs, others went to extremes to keep young criminals out of their communities. In the 1990s one community in California sought and received a legal injunction to keep gang members from associating with each other in public places. While the neighbors claimed that they once again felt safe in their homes, other felt that such injunctions seriously infringed on the civil rights of individuals.

The issue of how to deal with youthful offenders has been debated by the United States Supreme Court on several occasions in the late 20th and early 21st centuries. Two of the most important rulings involved the cases of *Thompson v. Oklahoma* and *Roper v. Simmons*. Both cases involved adolescents that had committed murder while under the age of eighteen. In both cases, the two boys were tried as adults and sentenced to death.

Their lawyers appealed these rulings all the way to the Supreme Court. In both cases, the court found that handing down the death penalty to anyone under the age of eighteen to be cruel and unusual punishment. These rulings abolished the use of the death penalty for minors.

Even though these two rulings have not been overturned, some people still believe that children that commit adult crimes should receive adult punishments.

The Birth of America's Juvenile Justice System

Howard N. Snyder and Melissa Sickmund

The Juvenile Justice System was established in 1899 to rehabilitate youthful offenders. At this time, many people believed that juveniles were more receptive to rehabilitation than adult criminals. The creators of the system determined that youthful offenders should be sentenced according to their ability to be rehabilitated instead of punished according to their offense. But as youth violence continued and the offenders' crimes became increasingly heinous in the latter half of the twentieth century, there was a shift in society's perception of juvenile delinquents. Many people questioned where there was any hope of reforming these children so that they would be fit to reenter the world. Citizens clamored for harsher penalties for young people that commit acts of violence. In the following selection, Howard N. Snyder and Melissa Sickmund explore the history of the juvenile justice system and how it has changed over the years. Snyder and Sickmund focus on how methods of dealing with offenders have shifted from rehabilitation to punishment and deterrence in the century since the system's inception. Snyder and Sickmund work for the National Center for Juvenile Justice.

The juvenile justice system was founded on the concept of rehabilitation through individualized justice.

Early in U.S. history, children who broke the law were treated the same as adult criminals.

Throughout the late 18th century, "infants" below the age of reason (traditionally age 7) were presumed to be incapable of criminal intent and were, therefore, exempt from prosecu-

Howard N. Snyder and Melissa Sickmund, "Juvenile Justice System Structure and Practice," *Juvenile Offenders and Victims: 1999 National Report*. Washington, DC: U.S. Department of Justice, Office of Justice Programs, Office of Juvenile Justice and Delinquency Prevention, 1999.

tion and punishment. Children as young as 7, however, could stand trial in criminal court for offenses committed and, if found guilty, could be sentenced to prison or even to death.

The 19th-century movement that led to the establishment of the juvenile court in the U.S. had its roots in 16th-century European educational reform movements. These earlier reform movements changed the perception of children from one of miniature adults to one of persons with less than fully developed moral and cognitive capacities.

As early as 1825, the Society for the Prevention of Juvenile Delinquency was advocating the separation of juvenile and adult offenders. Soon, facilities exclusively for juveniles were established in most major cities. By mid-century, these privately operated youth "prisons" were under criticism for various abuses. Many States then took on the responsibility of operating juvenile facilities.

The First Juvenile Court

The first juvenile court in this country was established in Cook County, Illinois, in 1899.

Illinois passed the Juvenile Court Act of 1899, which established the Nation's first juvenile court. The British doctrine of *parens patriae* (the State as parent) was the rationale for the right of the State to intervene in the lives of children in a manner different from the way it intervenes in the lives of adults. The doctrine was interpreted to mean that, because children were not of full legal capacity, the State had the inherent power and responsibility to provide protection for children whose natural parents were not providing appropriate care or supervision. A key element was the focus on the welfare of the child. Thus, the delinquent child was also seen as in need of the court's benevolent intervention.

Juvenile courts flourished for the first half of the 20th century.

By 1910, 32 States had established juvenile courts and/or probation services. By 1925, all but two States had followed suit. Rather than merely punishing delinquents for their crimes, juvenile courts sought to turn delinquents into productive citizens—through treatment.

The mission to help children in trouble was stated clearly in the laws that established juvenile courts. This benevolent mission led to procedural and substantive differences between the juvenile and criminal justice systems.

During the next 50 years, most juvenile courts had exclusive original jurisdiction over all youth under age 18 who were charged with violating criminal laws. Only if the juvenile court waived its jurisdiction in a case could a child be transferred to criminal court and tried as an adult. Transfer decisions were made on a case-by-case basis using a "best interests of the child and public" standard, and were thus within the realm of individualized justice.

Rehabilitation, Not Punishment

The focus on offenders and not offenses, on rehabilitation and not punishment, had substantial procedural impact.

Unlike the criminal justice system, where district attorneys select cases for trial, the juvenile court controlled its own intake. And unlike criminal prosecutors, juvenile court intake considered extra-legal as well as legal factors in deciding how to handle cases. Juvenile court intake also had discretion to handle cases informally, bypassing judicial action. . . .

In the courtroom, juvenile court hearings were much less formal than criminal court proceedings. In this benevolent court—with the express purpose of protecting children—due process protections afforded criminal defendants were deemed unnecessary. In the early juvenile courts, and even in some to this day, attorneys for the State and the youth are not considered essential to the operation of the system, especially in less serious cases.

A range of dispositional options was available to a judge wanting to help rehabilitate a child. Regardless of offense, outcomes ranging from warnings to probation supervision to training school confinement could be part of the treatment plan. Dispositions were tailored to "the best interests of the child." Treatment lasted until the child was "cured" or became an adult (age 21), whichever came first.

Can Youth Be Rehabilitated?

As public confidence in the treatment model waned, due process protections were introduced.

In the 1950's and 1960's, many came to question the ability of the juvenile court to succeed in rehabilitating delinquent youth. The treatment techniques available to juvenile justice professionals never reached the desired levels of effectiveness. Although the goal of rehabilitation through individualized justice—the basic philosophy of the juvenile justice system—was not in question, professionals were concerned about the growing number of juveniles institutionalized indefinitely in the name of treatment.

In a series of decisions beginning in the 1960's, the U.S. Supreme Court required that juvenile courts become more formal—more like criminal courts. Formal hearings were now required in waiver situations, and delinquents facing possible confinement were given protection against self-incrimination and rights to receive notice of the charges against them, to present witnesses, to question witnesses, and to have an attorney. Proof "beyond a reasonable doubt" rather than merely "a preponderance of evidence" was now required for an adjudication. The Supreme Court, however, still held that there were enough "differences of substance between the criminal and juvenile courts . . . to hold that a jury is not required in the latter. . . ."

Meanwhile Congress, in the Juvenile Delinquency Prevention and Control Act of 1968, recommended that children charged with noncriminal (status) offenses be handled outside the court system. A few years later, Congress passed the Juvenile Justice and Delinquency Prevention Act of 1974, which as a condition for State participation in the Formula Grants program required deinstitutionalization of status offenders and nonoffenders as well as the separation of juvenile delinquents from adult offenders. (In the 1980 amendments to the 1974 Act, Congress added a requirement that juveniles be removed from adult jail and lockup facilities.) Community-based programs, diversion, and deinstitutionalization became the banners of juvenile justice policy in the 1970's.

Harsher Punishment for Young Offenders

In the 1980's, the pendulum began to swing toward law and order.

During the 1980's, the public perceived that serious juvenile crime was increasing and that the system was too lenient with offenders. Although there was substantial misperception regarding increases in juvenile crime, many States responded by passing more punitive laws. Some laws removed certain classes of offenders from the juvenile justice system and handled them as adult criminals in criminal court. Others required the juvenile justice system to be more like the criminal justice system and to treat certain classes of juvenile offenders as criminals but in juvenile court.

As a result, offenders charged with certain offenses are *excluded* from juvenile court jurisdiction or face *mandatory* or *automatic waiver* to criminal court. In some States, concurrent jurisdiction provisions give prosecutors the discretion to file certain juvenile cases directly in criminal court rather than juvenile court. In some States, some adjudicated juvenile offenders face *mandatory sentences*.

The 1990's have been a time of unprecedented change as State legislatures crack down on juvenile crime. . . .

The 1980's and 1990's have seen significant change in terms of treating more juvenile offenders as criminals. Recently, States have been attempting to strike a balance in their juvenile justice systems among system and offender accountability, offender competency development, and community protection. Juvenile code purpose clauses also incorporate restorative justice language (offenders repair the harm done to victims and communities and accept responsibility for their criminal actions). Many States have added to the purpose clauses of their juvenile codes phrases such as:

- Hold juveniles accountable for criminal behavior.

- Provide effective deterrents.

- Protect the public from criminal activity.

- Balance attention to offenders, victims, and the community.

- Impose punishment consistent with the seriousness of the crime. . . .

No Difference Between Juveniles and Criminals

The juvenile justice system differs from the criminal justice system, but there is common ground.

The juvenile justice system grew out of the criminal justice system.

After working within the criminal justice system, designers of the juvenile justice system retained many of the components of the criminal justice system as they constructed a new process to respond to delinquent youth. . . .

During its nearly 100-year history, the juvenile justice system in the U.S. has seen fundamental changes in certain aspects of process and philosophy. Recently, there has been some discussion about the possibility of essentially merging the juvenile and criminal systems. . . .

Many States have changed the boundaries of juvenile court jurisdiction.

Traditionally, discretionary judicial waiver was the transfer mechanism on which most States relied. Beginning in the 1970's and continuing through the present, however, State legislatures have increasingly moved juvenile offenders into criminal court based on age and/or offense seriousness. . . .

In most States, juveniles convicted in criminal court cannot be tried in juvenile court for subsequent offenses.

In 31 States, juveniles who have been tried as adults must be prosecuted in criminal court for any subsequent offenses. Nearly all of these "once an adult/always an adult" provisions require that the youth must have been convicted of the offenses that triggered the initial criminal prosecution. . . .

A trend away from traditional juvenile dispositions is emerging.

Juvenile court dispositions were traditionally based on the offender's individual characteristics and situation. Dispositions were frequently indeterminate and generally had rehabilitation as a primary goal. As many States have shifted the purpose of juvenile court away from rehabilitation and toward punishment, accountability, and public safety, the emerging trend is toward dispositions based more on the offense than the offender. Offense-based dispositions tend to be determinate and proportional to the offense; retribution and deterrence replace rehabilitation as the primary goal.

The Gang Injunction Controversy in California

Julie Gannon Shoop

In the early 1990s, the residents of the Rocksprings section of San Jose, California, lived in fear of youth gang violence. Their streets were overrun by drug dealers and vandals. Children could not play in their own front yards and members of the community feared that their personal safety would be put in jeopardy if they reported gang members' behavior to the police. Citizens were able to reclaim their neighborhood after a civil injunction barred gang members, suspected or confirmed, from congregating in public or even wearing colors associated with certain gangs. In the following article, Julie Gannon Shoop explains how this controversial plan caused a stir across the country. Local prosecutors in San Jose saw the injunction as a breakthrough in the fight against youth violence. However, civil rights activists viewed the ordinance as a violation of individuals' First Amendment rights. Activists also worry that such injunctions could lead to an abuse of power on the part of the police, as well as discrimination against ethnic groups. Shoop explores the legality of such action and questions how effective the ordinance really is in keeping the streets safe. Shoop is editor of Trial, *the Association of Trial Lawyers of America's magazine.*

[S everal years ago,] residents of the Rocksprings area of San Jose, California, lived in fear. A four-square-block neighborhood claimed as gang turf, Rocksprings resembled—as the state supreme court would later put it—"an urban war zone."

Residents kept their children locked indoors. Loud music, foul language, and gunfire echoed in the streets. Sidewalks and

Julie Gannon Shoop, "Gang Warfare: Legal Battle Pits Personal Liberty against Public Safety," Trial, vol. 34, March 1998, pp. 12–15. Copyright 1998 American Association for Justice (formerly Association of Trial Lawyers of America). Reproduced by permission.

garage doors doubled as urinals. And citizens risked violent retaliation from gang members if they complained to police about rampant drug dealing, vandalism, and harassment.

Things have changed in Rocksprings. Crime rates have plummeted. The streets are cleaner. Kids play on lawns.

San Jose police and prosecutors say the change is the result of a 1993 civil injunction—granted by a judge under California's public nuisance statute—prohibiting gang members from congregating in public in Rocksprings and harassing or intimidating residents. Among other things, the injunction bars 38 named members of a Latino gang from "standing, sitting, walking, driving, gathering, or appearing anywhere in public view with any other defendant . . . or with any other known [gang] member."

The injunction brought "an overnight result," said City Attorney Joan Gallo. "After the injunction was served, immediately people began to come out of their homes again, and gang members disappeared from the area. The problem essentially went away."

The Price of Protection

But at what cost? Opponents of the Rocksprings injunction and the 20 or so others that courts have granted in California say that if public order is enhanced—and that, they claim, is debatable—it is at the expense of individual liberties guaranteed by the Constitution.

"We could have maximum public order if there were no Bill of Rights," said Erwin Chemerinsky, a law professor and constitutional scholar at the University of Southern California (USC). The Illinois Supreme Court agreed with that view [recently] when it struck down a Chicago city ordinance similar to the California injunctions.

In essence, gang injunctions are preemptive strikes against gang activity. They have become the weapon of choice for prosecutors in California, where law enforcement officials are contending with nearly 5,000 gangs and more than 250,000 gang members, far more than in any other state, according to a recent Justice Department survey. California prosecutors and defense attorneys said they are unaware of gang injunctions being issued elsewhere.

Injunctions generally prohibit the named defendants from engaging in both illegal conduct and otherwise lawful activities within certain geographical boundaries. In addition to barring gang members from gathering in public, some injunctions prohibit them from wearing gang colors or symbols and possessing everyday items like cellular phones, pagers, tools, and spray paint cans—objects they typically use to conduct drug sales or vandalize property.

"The injunction is an extremely valuable tool," said Michael Genelin, a deputy district attorney for Los Angeles County who heads the county's Hardcore Gang Unit. "It allows us to go after the gang as a whole, rather than individual gang members. Criminal conduct [by gangs] is group conduct, and there has to be a tool that will in some way stop the group action."

Public defenders and the American Civil Liberties Union (ACLU) have been fighting gang injunctions since the first one was granted [over] a decade ago. [In 1997,] the issue was addressed by the California Supreme Court, which upheld the Rocksprings injunction as constitutional. The U.S. Supreme Court declined to hear the case.

An appeals court had thrown out all or parts of 15 of the injunction's original 25 provisions. San Jose officials appealed only two to the supreme court: the provision prohibiting gang members from appearing together in public and one barring them from harassing or threatening residents who complained about gang activities.

On balance, the court held, the public interest in community safety and tranquility far outweighs concerns about narrow restrictions on freedoms for a few known lawbreakers.

"To hold that the liberty of the peaceful, industrious residents of Rocksprings must be forfeited to preserve the illusion of freedom for those whose ill conduct is deleterious to the community as a whole is to ignore half the political promise of the Constitution and the whole of its sense," Justice Janice Brown wrote for the court majority.

"Preserving the peace is the first duty of government, and it is for the protection of the community from the predations of the idle, the contentious, and the brutal that government was invented," Brown said.

The court rejected arguments by the ACLU's Northern California affiliate that the injunction was vague and over-broad and violated the gang members' First Amendment rights of speech and association. But Justice Stanley Mosk, in a vigorous dissent, said the defendants' freedom to associate with one another should not be limited when they are not committing crimes.

"The majority would permit our cities to close off entire neighborhoods to Latino youths who have done nothing more than dress in blue or black clothing or associate with others who do so; they would authorize criminal penalties for ordinary, nondisruptive acts of walking or driving through a residential neighborhood with a relative or friend," Mosk wrote. "In my view, such a blunderbuss approach amounts to both bad law and bad policy."

Chemerinsky of USC was "enormously troubled" by the decision. "What it does in practical effect is make people of a certain race suspect when they're in public places," he said. He added that the decision will likely lead courts to grant injunctions that cover more people and larger areas. "It opens the door to fairly large restrictions on freedom," he said.

Abuse of Discretion?

In the Illinois case, the state supreme court expressed a similar concern about discriminatory enforcement of the city's gang loitering ordinance.

The 1992 ordinance authorized police officers to disperse any group of two or more people "loitering" in a public place if the officer "reasonably believes" that at least one person is a gang member. Between 1992 and 1995, when an appeals court struck down the ordinance as unconstitutional, the law resulted in about 43,000 arrests of people—some gang members, some not—who refused to obey police orders to move along.

The state supreme court affirmed the appeals court decision . . . holding that the ordinance violated due process rights because of its vague definitions of terms and its "arbitrary restriction on personal liberties."

Ordinances like Chicago's "are drafted in an intentionally vague manner so that persons who are undesirable in the eyes of police and prosecutors can be convicted even though they are not chargeable with any other particular offense," Justice John Nickels wrote for the court. He said the law gave police officers "absolute discretion" to decide who was a gang member and what activities constituted loitering, providing ample opportunity for abuse.

The city has asked the Supreme Court to hear the case. Lawrence Rosenthal, Chicago deputy corporation counsel, said the petition to the Court disputes the finding that the ordinance is vague and demonstrates the law's effectiveness at reducing crime in gang-plagued areas of the city.

"What this case really comes down to is this: Is it irrational to prohibit loitering by groups containing criminal street gang members?" Rosenthal said. "We think the devastating effects of permitting a visibly lawless and disruptive element to dominate the public way make it very clear why a prohibition on gang loitering is eminently reasonable."

Questions about Effectiveness

Civil rights advocates dispute the assertion that injunctions accomplish what they set out to do. [In 1997,] the ACLU of

Southern California published a study finding that in at least one injunction area, violent crime actually increased in the months immediately after the injunction was issued and rose sharply in adjacent neighborhoods.

Elizabeth Schroeder, associate director of the Southern California ACLU, said the organization's analysis leads to two conclusions: that the named defendants moved to other areas to conduct their gang activities and that other gangsters moved into the vacated community.

An injunction "gives people in gang-infested areas a false hope that these injunctions are a panacea to stop crime," Schroeder said. "What we need to do is go back to the kinds of social programs that address the origins of gang problems," particularly education programs and job training for at-risk youths.

Genelin of Los Angeles County's Hardcore Gang Unit conceded that there might be "some minor displacement" of gang members to other areas. "But it is much more difficult for them when they leave their home turf," he said. "They can't operate with the same impunity" because rival gangs more often than not control other neighborhoods.

Since Acuna, though, the debate about effectiveness is, legally speaking, beside the point. Since obtaining the California Supreme Court's stamp of approval, prosecutors seeking injunctions are having an easier time of it.

Acuna "created a different atmosphere for us in the courts. The judges are more relaxed" about granting the orders, said Genelin, who last August obtained what has been called the most ambitious injunction to date against more than 50 members of the 18th Street Gang, one of Los Angeles's most notorious bands of criminals.

Although the ACLU has stopped challenging gang injunctions in court, its lawyers will continue to monitor the orders to see that they comport with the rules outlined in Acuna.

"Some of the injuctions may have language in them that even the California Supreme Court would find was unconstitutionally vague," Schroeder said.

And at least one new constitutional challenge is in the works. In [1998], the San Diego County public defender's office announced it would represent an alleged gang member named in an injunction granted [in December of 1997.]

Deputy Public Defender DawnElla Gilzean said her client plans to challenge several provisions of the injunction that are nearly identical to provisions in the Rocksprings injunction. These provisions were struck down by the appeals court but were not considered by the supreme court. These include, for example, sections that ban wearing gang symbols and possessing marker pens, razor blades, pagers, and other objects.

"You can do an injunction right," Gilzean acknowledged, but she contends San Diego's way is wrong.

The details may yet need hammering out, but civil rights advocates seem resigned that injunctions have become a fixture in California's antigang efforts. And injunction proponents are unapologetic about restricting gang members' freedoms.

"There is an unwritten contract you have with people in your community, and that is to act in a way that [promotes] the general well-being of the community," said Genelin. When that contract is broken and the community suffers, he said, claims for constitutional protection ring hollow.

Juvenile Executions Prohibited for Defendants Under the Age of Fifteen

John Paul Stevens

In the early 1980s, William Wayne Thompson helped three older men murder his former brother-in-law, Charles Keene. The motivation for the crime was the physical abuse that Keene had inflicted on Thompson's older sister during their marriage. Thompson admitted his guilt to several people, telling them that he had stabbed and shot Keene and then dumped his body in a nearby river. At the time of the incident, Thompson was only fifteen years old. The prosecuting attorney filed a petition to have Thompson tried as an adult, due to the brutality of the crime. The petition was granted. Thompson was found guilty and sentenced to death. Thompson's lawyers appealed the decision, arguing that sentencing a minor to death was a violation of the Eighth Amendment's protection against cruel and unusual punishment. After the case was heard by several state courts, it was eventually sent to the Supreme Court of the United States. In the following excerpt, Justice John Paul Stevens outlines the court's decision. A careful review of the facts was conducted. In a five to three vote, with one judge abstaining, the court ultimately ruled that executing a minor is unconstitutional and violated the defendant's Eighth Amendment rights.

[T]he] Petitioner, when he was 15 years old, actively participated in a brutal murder. Because petitioner was a "child" as a matter of Oklahoma law, the District Attorney filed a statutory petition seeking to have him tried as an adult, which the trial court granted. He was then convicted and sentenced to death, and the Court of Criminal Appeals of Oklahoma affirmed.

John Paul Stevens, writing for the majority, U.S. Supreme Court, *Thompson v. Oklahoma*, 487 U.S. 815, 1988.

JUSTICE [John Paul] STEVENS, joined by JUSTICE [William J.] BRENNAN, JUSTICE [Thurgood] MARSHALL, and JUSTICE [Harry] BLACKMUN, concluded that the "cruel and unusual punishments" prohibition of the Eighth Amendment, made applicable to the States by the Fourteenth Amendment, prohibits the execution of a person who was under 16 years of age at the time of his or her offense.

JUSTICE STEVENS announced the judgment of the Court and delivered an opinion in which JUSTICE BRENNAN, JUSTICE MARSHALL, and JUSTICE BLACKMUN join:

The Details of the Case

Because there is no claim that the punishment would be excessive if the crime had been committed by an adult, only a brief statement of facts is necessary. In concert with three older persons, petitioner actively participated in the brutal murder of his former brother-in-law in the early morning hours of January 23, 1983. The evidence disclosed that the victim had been shot twice, and that his throat, chest, and abdomen had been cut. He also had multiple bruises and a broken leg. His body had been chained to a concrete block and thrown into a river where it remained for almost four weeks. Each of the four participants was tried separately and each was sentenced to death.

Because petitioner was a "child" as a matter of Oklahoma law, the District Attorney filed a statutory petition seeking an order finding "that said child is competent and had the mental capacity to know and appreciate the wrongfulness of his [conduct]." After a hearing, the trial court concluded "that there are virtually no reasonable prospects for rehabilitation of William Wayne Thompson within the juvenile system and that William Wayne Thompson should be held accountable for his acts as if he were an adult and should be certified to stand trial as an adult. . . ."

At the penalty phase of the trial, the prosecutor asked the jury to find two aggravating circumstances: that the murder was especially heinous, atrocious, or cruel; and that there was a probability that the defendant would commit criminal acts of violence that would constitute a continuing threat to society. The jury found the first, but not the second, and fixed petitioner's punishment at death.

The Court of Criminal Appeals affirmed the conviction and sentence, citing its earlier opinion in Eddings v. State for the proposition that "once a minor is certified to stand trial as an adult, he may also, without violating the Constitution, be punished as an adult." We granted *certiorari* [a review of the case] to consider whether a sentence of death is cruel and unusual punishment for a crime committed by a 15-year-old child. . . .

Children and Adults Are Different in the Eyes of the Law

Justice Powell has repeatedly reminded us of the importance of "the experience of mankind, as well as the long history of our law, recognizing that there are differences which must be accommodated in determining the rights and duties of children as compared with those of adults. Examples of this distinction abound in our law: in contracts, in torts, in criminal law and procedure, in criminal sanctions and rehabilitation, and in the right to vote and to hold office." Oklahoma recognizes this basic distinction in a number of its statutes. Thus, a minor is not eligible to vote, to sit on a jury, to marry without parental consent, or to purchase alcohol or cigarettes. Like all other States, Oklahoma has developed a juvenile justice system in which most offenders under the age of 18 are not held criminally responsible. Its statutes do provide, however, that a 16- or 17-year-old charged with murder and other serious felonies shall be considered an adult. Other than the special certification procedure that was used to authorize petitioner's trial in this case "as an adult," apparently there are no Oklahoma statutes, either civil or criminal, that treat a person under 16 years of age as anything but a "child."

The line between childhood and adulthood is drawn in different ways by various States. There is, however, complete or near unanimity among all 50 States and the District of Columbia in treating a person under 16 as a minor for several important purposes. In no State may a 15-year-old vote or serve on a jury. Further, in all but one State a 15-year-old may not drive without parental consent, and in all but four States a 15-year-old may not marry without parental consent. Additionally, in those States that have legislated on the subject, no one under age 16 may purchase pornographic materials (50 States), and in most States that have some form of legalized gambling, minors are not permitted to participate without parental consent (42 States). Most relevant, however, is the fact that all States have enacted legislation designating the maximum age for juvenile court jurisdiction at no less than 16. All of this legislation is consistent with the experience of mankind, as well as the long history of our law, that the normal 15-year-old is not prepared to assume the full responsibilities of an adult.

Most state legislatures have not expressly confronted the question of establishing a minimum age for imposition of the death penalty. In 14 States, capital punishment is not authorized at all, and in 19 others capital punishment is authorized but no minimum age is expressly stated in the death penalty statute. One might argue on the basis of this body of legislation that there is no chronological age at which the imposition of the death penalty is unconstitutional and that our current standards of decency would still tolerate the execution of 10-year-old children. We think it self-evident that such an argument is unacceptable; indeed, no such argument has been advanced in this case. If, therefore, we accept the premise that some offenders are simply too young to be put to death, it is reasonable to put this group of statutes to one side because they do not focus on the question of where the chronological age line should be drawn. When we confine our attention to the 18 States that have expressly established a minimum age in their death penalty statutes, we find that all of them require that the defendant have attained at least the age of 16 at the time of the capital offense.

The conclusion that it would offend civilized standards of decency to execute a person who was less than 16 years old at the time of his or her offense is consistent with the views that have been expressed by respected professional organizations, by other nations that share our Anglo-American heritage, and by the leading members of the Western European community. Thus, the American Bar Association and the American Law Institute have formally expressed their opposition to the death penalty for juveniles. . . .

What is the Proper Punishment?

It is generally agreed "that punishment should be directly related to the personal culpability of the criminal defendant." California v. Brown. There is also broad agreement on the proposition that adolescents as a class are less mature and responsible than adults. We stressed this difference in explaining the importance of treating the defendant's youth as a mitigating factor in capital cases:

> But youth is more than a chronological fact. It is a time and condition of life when a person may be most susceptible to influence and to psychological damage. Our history is replete with laws and judicial recognition that minors, especially in their earlier years, generally are less mature and responsible than adults. Particularly "during the formative years of childhood and adolescence, minors often lack the experience, perspective, and judgment" expected of adults.

To add further emphasis to the special mitigating force of youth, Justice Powell quoted the following passage from the

1978 Report of the Twentieth Century Fund Task Force on Sentencing Policy Toward Young Offenders:

> [A]dolescents, particularly in the early and middle teen years, are more vulnerable, more impulsive, and less self-disciplined than adults. Crimes committed by youths may be just as harmful to victims as those committed by older persons, but they deserve less punishment because adolescents may have less capacity to control their conduct and to think in long-range terms than adults. Moreover, youth crime as such is not exclusively the offender's fault; offenses by the young also represent a failure of family, school, and the social system, which share responsibility for the development of America's youth.

Thus, the Court has already endorsed the proposition that less culpability should attach to a crime committed by a juvenile than to a comparable crime committed by an adult. The basis for this conclusion is too obvious to require extended explanation. Inexperience, less education, and less intelligence make the teenager less able to evaluate the consequences of his or her conduct while at the same time he or she is much more apt to be motivated by mere emotion or peer pressure than is an adult. The reasons why juveniles are not trusted with the privileges and responsibilities of an adult also explain why their irresponsible conduct is not as morally reprehensible as that of an adult.

> "The death penalty is said to serve two principal social purposes: retribution and deterrence of capital crimes by prospective offenders." In Gregg we concluded that as "an expression of society's moral outrage at particularly offensive conduct," retribution was not "inconsistent with our respect for the dignity of men." Given the lesser culpability of the juvenile offender, the teenager's capacity for growth, and society's fiduciary obligations to its children, this conclusion is simply inapplicable to the execution of a 15-year-old offender.

For such a young offender, the deterrence rationale is equally unacceptable. The Department of Justice statistics indicate that about 98% of the arrests for willful homicide involved persons who were over 16 at the time of the offense. Thus, excluding younger persons from the class that is eligible for the death penalty will not diminish the deterrent value of capital punishment for the vast majority of potential offenders. And even with respect to those under 16 years of age, it is obvious that the potential deterrent value of the death sentence is insignificant for two reasons. The likelihood that the teenage offender has made the kind of cost-benefit analysis that attaches any weight to the possibility of execution is so remote as to be virtually nonexistent. And, even if one posits such a cold-blooded calculation by a 15-year-old, it is fanciful to believe that he would be deterred by the knowledge that a small number of persons his age have been executed during the 20th century. In short, we are not persuaded that the imposition of the death penalty for offenses committed by persons under 16 years of age has made, or can be expected to make, any measurable contribution to the goals that capital punishment is intended to achieve. It is, therefore, "nothing more than the purposeless and needless imposition of pain and suffering," and thus an unconstitutional punishment.

Petitioner's counsel and various *amici curiae* [friends of the court] have asked us to "draw a line" that would prohibit the execution of any person who was under the age of 18 at the time of the offense. Our task today, however, is to decide the case before us; we do so by concluding that the Eighth and Fourteenth Amendments prohibit the execution of a person who was under 16 years of age at the time of his or her offense.

The judgment of the Court of Criminal Appeals is *vacated*, [made legally void] and the case is *remanded*; [sent back to lower court] with instructions to enter an appropriate order vacating petitioner's death sentence.

It is so ordered.

An End to Juvenile Executions in the United States

Anthony Kennedy

In 2005, the Supreme Court of the United States once again examined the question of whether juvenile offenders can receive the death penalty. In 1993, seventeen-year-old Christopher Simmons hatched a plan to commit robbery and murder. Along with two younger friends, Simmons broke into the home of Shirley Crook. The boys tied the woman up with duct tape and threw her in the back of a van. They drove towards a state park where they threw the woman off of a bridge. Simmons later confessed to the crime and even reenacted the events for the police. The jury convicted Simmons of first-degree murder and sentenced him to death. Simmons' lawyers appealed the sentence, arguing that the young man's age at the time of the crime should exempt him from the death penalty. The case made its way all the way to the Supreme Court of the United States. The justices considered the decisions made in Thompson v. Oklahoma, *as well as other cases, to try to come to a final decision concerning the death penalty and persons under the age of eighteen. In a five to four decision, the court ruled that capital punishment for juveniles was considered cruel and unusual punishment, violating the Eighth Amendment. Justice Anthony Kennedy wrote for the majority.*

Justice [Anthony] Kennedy: delivered the opinion of the Court.

This case requires us to address, for the second time in a decade and a half, whether it is permissible under the Eighth and Fourteenth Amendments to the Constitution of the United States to execute a juvenile offender who was older

Anthony Kennedy, writing for the majority, U.S. Supreme Court, *Roper v. Simmons*, 513 U.S., 2005.

than 15 but younger than 18 when he committed a capital crime. We reconsider the question.

A Horrific Crime

At the age of 17, when he was still a junior in high school, Christopher Simmons, the respondent here, committed murder. About nine months later, after he had turned 18, he was tried and sentenced to death. There is little doubt that Simmons was the instigator of the crime. Before its commission Simmons said he wanted to murder someone. In chilling, callous terms he talked about his plan, discussing it for the most part with two friends, Charles Benjamin and John Tessmer, then aged 15 and 16 respectively. Simmons proposed to commit burglary and murder by breaking and entering, tying up a victim, and throwing the victim off a bridge. Simmons assured his friends they could "get away with it" because they were minors.

The three met at about 2 a.m. on the night of the murder, but Tessmer left before the other two set out. (The State later charged Tessmer with conspiracy, but dropped the charge in exchange for his testimony against Simmons.) Simmons and Benjamin entered the home of the victim, Shirley Crook, after reaching through an open window and unlocking the back door. Simmons turned on a hallway light. Awakened, Mrs. Crook called out, "Who's there?" In response Simmons entered Mrs. Crook's bedroom, where he recognized her from a previous car accident involving them both. Simmons later admitted this confirmed his resolve to murder her.

Using duct tape to cover her eyes and mouth and bind her hands, the two perpetrators put Mrs. Crook in her minivan and drove to a state park. They reinforced the bindings, covered her head with a towel, and walked her to a railroad trestle spanning the Meramec River. There they tied her hands and feet together with electrical wire, wrapped her whole face in duct tape and threw her from the bridge, drowning her in the waters below. . . .

[After] receiving information of Simmons' involvement, police arrested him at his high school and took him to the police station in Fenton, Missouri. They read him his *Miranda* rights. Simmons waived his right to an attorney and agreed to answer questions. After less than two hours of interrogation, Simmons confessed to the murder and agreed to perform a videotaped reenactment at the crime scene.

The State charged Simmons with burglary, kidnaping, stealing, and murder in the first degree. . . . He was tried as an adult. At trial the State introduced Simmons' confession and the videotaped reenactment of the crime, along with testimony that Simmons discussed the crime in advance and bragged about it later. The defense called no witnesses in the guilt phase. The jury having returned a verdict of murder, the trial proceeded to the penalty phase.

The State sought the death penalty. As aggravating factors, the State submitted that the murder was committed for the purpose of receiving money; was committed for the purpose of avoiding, interfering with, or preventing lawful arrest of the defendant; and involved depravity of mind and was outrageously and wantonly vile, horrible, and inhuman. The State called Shirley Crook's husband, daughter, and two sisters, who presented moving evidence of the devastation her death had brought to their lives. . . .

A Question of Age

During closing arguments, both the prosecutor and defense counsel addressed Simmons' age, which the trial judge had instructed the jurors they could consider as a mitigating factor. Defense counsel reminded the jurors that juveniles of Simmons' age cannot drink, serve on juries, or even see certain movies, because "the legislatures have wisely decided that individuals of a certain age aren't responsible enough." Defense counsel argued that Simmons' age should make "a huge difference to [the jurors] in deciding just exactly what sort of punishment to make." In rebuttal, the prosecutor gave the following response: "Age, he says. Think about age. Seventeen years old. Isn't that scary? Doesn't that scare you? Mitigating? Quite the contrary I submit. Quite the contrary."

The jury recommended the death penalty after finding the State had proved each of the three aggravating factors submitted to it. Accepting the jury's recommendation, the trial judge imposed the death penalty.

Simmons obtained new counsel, who moved in the trial court to set aside the conviction and sentence. One argument was that Simmons had received ineffective assistance at trial. To support this contention, the new counsel called as witnesses Simmons' trial attorney, Simmons' friends and neighbors, and clinical psychologists who had evaluated him. . . .

After these proceedings in Simmons' case had run their course, this Court held that the Eighth and Fourteenth Amendments prohibit the execution of a mentally retarded person. Simmons filed a new petition for state postconviction relief, arguing that the reasoning of *Atkins* established that the Constitution prohibits the execution of a juvenile who was under 18 when the crime was committed.

The Missouri Supreme Court agreed. . . .

[The court] set aside Simmons' death sentence and resentenced him to "life imprisonment without eligibility for probation, parole, or release except by act of the Governor. . . ."

We granted *certiorari* [a review of the case], 540 U. S. 1160 (2004), and now affirm. . . .

A Matter of Public Opinion

The prohibition against "cruel and unusual punishments," like other expansive language in the Constitution, must be interpreted according to its text, by considering history, tradition, and precedent, and with due regard for its purpose and function in the constitutional design. To implement this framework we have established the propriety and affirmed the necessity of referring to "the evolving standards of decency that mark the progress of a maturing society" to determine which punishments are so disproportionate as to be cruel and unusual.

In *Thompson v. Oklahoma*, a plurality of the Court determined that our standards of decency do not permit the execution of any offender under the age of 16 at the time of the crime. . . .

As in *Atkins*, the objective indicia of consensus in this case—the rejection of the juvenile death penalty in the majority of States; the infrequency of its use even where it remains on the books; and the consistency in the trend toward abolition of the practice—provide sufficient evidence that today our society views juveniles, in the words *Atkins* used respecting the mentally retarded, as "categorically less culpable than the average criminal. . . ."

A Matter of Maturity

A central feature of death penalty is a particular assessment of the circumstances of the crime and the characteristics of the offender. The system is designed to consider both aggravating and mitigating circumstances, including youth, in every case. Given this Court's own insistence on individualized consideration, petitioner maintains that it is both arbitrary and unnecessary to adopt a categorical rule barring imposition of the death penalty on any offender under 18 years of age.

We disagree. The differences between juvenile and adult offenders are too marked and well understood to risk allowing a youthful person to receive the death penalty despite insufficient culpability. An unacceptable likelihood exists that the brutality or cold-blooded nature of any particular crime would overpower mitigating arguments based on youth as a matter of course, even where the juvenile offender's objective immaturity, vulnerability, and lack of true depravity should require a sentence less severe than death. In some cases a defendant's youth may even be counted against him. In this very case, as we noted above, the prosecutor argued Simmons' youth was aggravating rather than mitigating. While this sort of over-reaching could be corrected by a particular rule to ensure that the mitigating force of youth is not overlooked, that would not address our larger concerns.

It is difficult even for expert psychologists to differentiate between the juvenile offender whose crime reflects unfortunate yet transient immaturity, and the rare juvenile offender whose crime reflects irreparable corruption. As we understand it, this difficulty underlies the rule forbidding psychiatrists from diagnosing any patient under 18 as having antisocial personality disorder, a disorder also referred to as psychopathy or sociopathy, and which is characterized by callousness, cynicism, and contempt for the feelings, rights, and suffering of others. If trained psychiatrists with the advantage of clinical testing and observation refrain, despite diagnostic expertise, from assessing any juvenile under 18 as having antisocial personality disorder, we conclude that States should refrain from asking jurors to issue a far graver condemnation—that a juvenile offender merits the death penalty. When a juvenile offender commits a heinous crime, the State can exact forfeiture of some of the most basic liberties, but the State cannot extinguish his life and his potential to attain a mature understanding of his own humanity.

Drawing the line at 18 years of age is subject, of course, to the objections always raised against categorical rules. The qualities that distinguish juveniles from adults do not disappear when an individual turns 18. By the same token, some under 18 have already attained a level of maturity some adults will never reach. For the reasons we have discussed, however, a line must be drawn. The plurality opinion in *Thompson* drew the line at 16. In the intervening years the *Thompson* plurality's conclusion that offenders under 16 may not be executed has not been challenged. The logic of *Thompson* extends to those who are under 18. The age of 18 is the point where society draws the line for many purposes between childhood and adulthood. It is, we conclude, the age at which the line for death eligibility ought to rest.

Chronology

Around 4000 B.C.

Biblical accounts claim that the first murder was committed by Cain, the son of Adam and Eve, who murdered his brother, Abel. Though specific ages for the brothers are not given, some accounts place the two in their late teens or early twenties.

1775–1783

During the American Revolution, gangs of young people began forming in and around large cities. Some historians argue that this was caused by the disappointment that many immigrants felt.

1874

In Boston, fourteen-year-old Jesse Pomeroy is arrested for the brutal murder of a four-year-old boy. It is later discovered that Pomeroy also killed a ten-year-old girl. Pomeroy was convicted and sentenced to death by hanging, but the governor refused his death warrant. The boy's sentence was later reduced to life in solitary confinement.

1875

Sixteen-year-old William H. Bonney, later known as Billy the Kid, shoots and kills blacksmith Frank Cahill. Billy is said to have killed twenty-one men, though historians argue that this number is probably closer to nine.

1899

The United States' first juvenile court is established in Chicago.

1909

The Juvenile Psychopathic Institute opens its doors to study youthful offenders. Dr. William Healy argued that juvenile delinquency might actually be a mental health problem. His research would contribute greatly to the understanding of the adolescent mind.

1924

Nineteen-year-old Nathan Leopold and eighteen-year-old Richard Loeb murder fourteen-year-old Bobby Franks. The killers were from wealthy families and were well-educated. Their crime changed many people's ideas about juvenile offenders.

1936

J. Edgar Hoover, director of the Federal Bureau of Investigation (FBI), gives a speech at the Chicago Boys' Club dinner. After an increase in juvenile crime during the Great Depression, Hoover calls upon the parents of the nation's children to guide them away from crime and violence.

The 1940s

Youth gangs increase in and around urban areas. Some of the gangs were said to have been defending their neighborhoods, while others were far more violent and frightening. Several gangs in New York and Boston assaulted and terrified Jewish adolescents while the police largely ignored these events.

1954

At a hearing of the Senate Subcommittee on Juvenile Delinquency, Dr. Fredric Wertham argues that fictional violence and crime in comic books has an effect on juvenile delinquency. The Comic Code Authority is formed to restrict explicit content in comic books as a result.

1964

Edward Kemper murders his grandparents. The young man is just fifteen at the time. He is committed to a state hospital for a time and then released into his mother's care. He would later go on to murder six college-aged women, his own mother, and his mother's friend.

1970

Frustrations over the war in Vietnam reach a boiling point. Students at campuses across the country rally for peace. Violence breaks out at and around several schools, including Kent State University in Ohio. The governor calls in the National Guard to keep the peace at an antiwar rally. Some protestors throw rocks at the guardsmen and after the crowd refuses to disperse the rally for peace falls into chaos. Shots ring out and four students are killed.

1979

Sixteen-year-old Brenda Spencer opens fire on the elementary school across the street from her house, wounding eight children and one adult and killing two men who were trying to protect the children. After a six-hour standoff with police, Spencer is taken into custody and questioned. When asked why she committed the crime, she replies, "I don't like Mondays."

The 1980s

The number of single-parent households in the United States increases in the 1980s. Some critics blame the breakdown of the American family for violence among youths. Others see the rise in popularity of rap and hip-hop music, with its sometimes violent lyrics, as having a negative impact on young fans.

1983

Fifteen-year-old Cindy Collier and fourteen-year-old Shirley Wolf brutally murder an elderly woman and then steal her car. After the two are arrested, the girls admit that they got "a kick" out of their crime.

1985

The Parents Music Resource Center (PMRC) is formed by four mothers in an effort to seek censorship of overly explicit music and establish a rating system for music. The group later disbands, but leaves a lasting impression on the music industry by creating a parental advisory sticker that is used to warn parents of albums containing references to violence, drugs, and sex.

1987

In Missouri, twelve-year-old Nathan Ferris is constantly teased about his weight by bullies at school. After a classmate humiliates him in front of other students, he shoots the other boy and then kills himself.

1988

The U.S. Supreme Court hands down a ruling in the case of *Thompson v. Oklahoma*. William Thompson was only fifteen years old when he murders his brother-in-law. He was tried as an adult and sentenced to death. His lawyers argue that sentencing a fifteen-year-old to death constitutes "cruel and unusual punishment," thus violating the Eighth Amendment. The Supreme Court agrees with Thompson's lawyers and overturns the boy's death sentence.

1989

Brothers Lyle and Erik Menendez murder their parents in order to inherit over two million dollars. The brothers are only nineteen and twenty-one when they commit the crime.

The 1990s

The mid- to late-1990s are marked by a series of school shootings across the country.

1990

The Center for Disease Control and Prevention develops the Youth Violence Risk Behavior Survey. The study finds that one in twenty high-school seniors had carried a firearm to school.

1993

An injunction passed in the Rocksprings community of San Jose, California, prevents suspected gang members from associating in public. Residents feel that the injunction will help to reduce youth violence, while civil rights advocates argue that it violates individuals' rights.

1998

In a rural area outside of Jonesboro, Arkansas, thirteen-year-old Mitchell Johnson and eleven-year-old Andrew Golden pull the fire alarms at the Westside Middle School and then open fire on students fleeing the building. Four students and one teacher are killed.

1999

Eric Harris and Dylan Klebold terrorize Columbine High School. The two boys murder twelve students and one teacher before taking their own lives.

2000

Six-year-old Dedrick Owens brings a gun to school and shoots classmate Kayla Rolland. The six-year-old girl dies at the scene and becomes the youngest victim of a school shooting.

March 1, 2005

In the case of *Roper v. Simmons*, the U.S. Supreme Court rules to abolish the death penalty for juvenile defendants who committed crimes while under the age of eighteen. Christopher Simmons is only seventeen when he helps two friends murder Shirley Crook.

March 21, 2005

Seventeen-year-old Jeffrey James Weise murders his grandfather and his grandfather's girlfriend, before heading to Red Lake High School where he kills seven people before taking his own life.

Organizations to Contact

The editors have compiled the following list of organizations concerned with the issues debated in this book. The descriptions are derived from materials provided by the organizations. All have publications or information available for interested readers. The list was compiled on the date of publication of the present volume; the information provided here may change. Be aware that many organizations take several weeks or longer to respond to inquiries, so allow as much time as possible.

Adults and Children Together Against Violence (ACT)
750 First Street NE, Washington, DC 20002
(202) 336-5817
e-mail: jsilva@apa.org
Web site: actagainstviolence.apa.org

The ACT is a prevention organization that focuses on helping adults be good role models for young children by teaching nonviolent methods or resolving conflicts and dealing with frustration. The organization's goal is to raise awareness about how adult behavior influences young children.

Centers for Disease Control and Prevention (CDC)
Mailstop K65, 4770 Buford Highway NE
Atlanta, GA 30341-3724
(770) 488-1506
e-mail: cdcinfo@cdc.gov
Web site: www.cdc.gov/ncipc

In 1992 the CDC established the National Center for Injury Prevention and Control (NCIPC). As the lead federal agency for injury prevention, the NCIPC provides statistics on youth violence, as well as strategies for prevention.

Center for the Prevention of School Violence (CPSV)
1801 Mail Service Center, Raleigh, NC 27699-1801

(800) 299-6054
e-mail: keesha.white@ncmail.net
Web site: www.ncdjjdp.org/cpsv

Established in 1993, the CPSV is a resource center that promotes efforts to support safer schools through understanding school violence and searching for solutions.

Center for the Study and Prevention of Violence (CSPV)
Institute of Behavioral Science
University of Colorado at Boulder, Boulder, CO   80302
(303) 492-1032
e-mail: cspv@colorado.edu
Web site: www.colorado.edu/cspv

The CSPV acts as an information house of literature on the causes of violence and forms of prevention. The organization offers blueprints for several different types of violence prevention programs.

Children's Defense Fund (CDF)
25 E Street NW, Washington, DC   20001
(202) 628-8787
e-mail: cdfinfo@childrensdefense.org
Web site: www.childrensdefense.org

The mission of the CDF is to ensure that every child is given a safe start in life and successful passage into adulthood. The organization promotes programs that work to keep children out of trouble and away from violence.

Institute for the Study and Prevention of Violence (ISPV)
230 Auditorium Building, Kent State University
Kent, Ohio   44242
(330) 672-7917
e-mail: ISPV@kent.edu
Web site: dept.kent.edu/violence

The ISVP was founded in 1998 to study the causes of violence and evaluate methods of prevention, including the training of law enforcement officials, teachers, and other professionals.

National School Safety Center (NSSC)
141 Duesenberg Drive, Suite 11, Westlake Village, CA   91362
(805) 373-9977
Web site: www.schoolsafety.us

The NSSC works towards the prevention of school violence and crime by providing parents, teachers, and students with information, resources, consultation, and training services.

**National Youth Violence Prevention
Resource Center (NYVPRC)**
PO Box 10809, Rockville, MD   20849-0809
e-mail: NYVPRC@safeyouth.org
Web site: www.safeyouth.org

NYVPRC provides professionals, parents, and students with current information pertaining to youth violence and offers tools to help resolve conflicts in a nonviolent manner, stop bullying, and prevent violence caused by or inflicted upon young people.

For Further Research

Books

Elijah Anderson, *Code of the Street: Decency, Violence and the Moral Life of the Inner City.* New York: W. W. Norton & Company, Inc., 1999.

Carol Anne Davis, *Children Who Kill: Profiles of Pre-teen and Teenage Killers.* London: Allison & Busby Limited, 2003.

Nancy E. Dowd, Dorothy G. Singer, and Robin Fretwell Wilson, eds., *Handbook of Children, Culture, and Violence.* Thousand Oaks, CA: Sage Publications, 2006.

Mark S. Fleisher, *Dead End Kids: Gang Girls and the Boys They Know.* Madison: University of Wisconsin Press, 2000.

Henry A. Giroux, *Fugitive Cultures: Race, Violence, and Youth.* New York: Routledge, 1996.

Lt. Col. Dave Grossman and Gloria DeGaetano, *Stop Teaching Our Kids to Kill: A Call to Action Against TV, Movie, and Video Game Violence.* New York: Crown Publishing, 1999.

Gerard Jones, *Killing Monsters: Why Children Need Fantasy, Super Heroes, and Make-Believe Violence.* New York: Basic Books, 2002.

Steven J. Kirsh, *Children, Adolescents, and Media Violence: A Critical Look at the Research.* Thousand Oaks, CA: Sage Publications, 2006.

Mike Males, *The Scapegoat Generation.* Monroe, ME: Common Courage Press, 1996.

Diane Ravitch and Joseph P. Viteritti, eds.), *Kid Stuff: Marketing Sex and Violence to America's Children*. Baltimore: John Hopkins University Press, 2003.

Anita Roberts, *Safe Teen: Powerful Alternatives to Violence*. Vancouver: Polestar, 2001.

Karen Sternheimer, *It's Not the Media: The Truth About Pop Culture's Influence on Children*. Boulder, CO: Westview Press, 2003.

David S. Tannenhaus, *Juvenile Justice in the Making*. New York: Oxford University Press, 2004.

Franklin E. Zimring, *American Youth Violence*. New York: Oxford University Press, 1998.

Periodicals

E. Bonham, "Adolescent Mental health and the Juvenile Justice System," *Pediatric Nursing*, November–December 2006.

T.L. Cheng, R. A. Brenner, J. L. Wright, H.C. Sachs, P. Moyer, and M.R. Rao, "Children's Violent Television Viewing: Are Parents Monitoring?" *Pediatrics*, July 2004.

Economist, "Breeding Evil? Defending Video Games," August 6, 2005.

David Greenberg, "Students Have Always Been Violent," *Slate*, May 7, 1999.

Duncan Greenberg, "Youth Violence, Media Silence: The Millenials," *Yale Herald*, February 9, 2007.

T. M. Kelley, "Preventing Youth Violence through Health Realization," *Youth Violence and Juvenile Justice*, vol. 1, issue 4, 2003.

R. C. Kramer, "Poverty, Inequality, and Youth Violence," *Annals of the American Academy of Political and Social Science*, January 2000.

S. F. Lambert, N.S. Ialongo, R. C. Boyd, and M.R. Cooley, "Risk Factors for Community Violence Exposure in Adolescence," *American Journal of Community Psychology*, September 2005.

M. D. Lemonick, "The Search for a Murder Gene," *Time*, January 20, 2003.

D. Lavers, "Media Violence: Ugly and Getting Uglier," *World & I*, March 2002.

J. M. MacDonald, A. R. Piquero, R. F. Valois, and K. J. Zullig, "The Relationship between Life Satisfaction, Risk-taking Behaviors, and Youth Violence," *Journal of Interpersonal Violence*, November 2005.

K. Y. Mack, M. J. Leiber, R. A. Featherstone, and M. A. Monserud, "Reassessing the Family-Delinquency Association: Do Family Type, Family Processes, and Economic Factors Make a Difference?" *Journal of Criminal Justice*, January–February 2007.

K. Reich, P. L. Culross, and R. E. Behrman, "Children, Youth, and Gun Violence: Analysis and Recommendations," *Future of Children*, Summer–Fall 2002.

J. W. Richardson, and K. A. Scott, "Rap Music and Its Violent Progeny: America's Culture of Violence in Context," *Journal of Negro Education*, Summer 2002, pp. 175–192.

Julie Scelfo, "Bad Girls Go Wild: A Rise in Girl-on-Girl Violence is Making Headlines and Prompting Scientists to Ask Why," *Newsweek*, June 13, 2005.

L. Ulanoff, "Who's Afraid of Mature Games?" *PC Magazine*, April 12, 2005.

A. Wilson, "The Bully Problem," *World & I*, vol. 21, issue 8, 2006.

Index